"Powerful and timely! Carmen Harra's way for authentic, reciprocal, passionate, ̶.̶.̶.̶ ̶.̶.̶.̶.̶.̶.̶.̶.̶ ̶.̶.̶.̶.̶.̶.̶.̶.̶.̶.̶ *Committed* is your user's guide to manifesting and designing deep heart-based connections through self-love. Dr. Harra gives our mind a reason to accept what our heart already knows—that love is the great healer of life. Within these pages you'll discover the miracle of commitment…an alchemic evolutionary journey for experiencing true love."

—Dr. Darren Weissman, bestselling author of
The Power of Infinite Love & Gratitude and developer of The LifeLine Technique®

"Harra's deep understanding of human nature and her insight into the seven main love archetypes are vital to readers who want to develop an authentic, impassioned relationship with their significant other."

—Iris Benrubi, relationship expert and bestselling
author of *Lonely and Single to Loved and Adored*

"With compassion and precision, Dr. Harra walks the reader through the confusing landscapes and minefields of online dating and real-time relationships. Her conversational style packs a lot of wise guidance on how to identify key relationship issues through understanding seven male archetypes: Independent, Workaholic, Narcissistic, Free Spirit, Hopeless Romantic, and Introvert. An archetype is a universal blueprint to the human personality regardless of nationality, ethnicity, race, religion, or culture. The brilliance in this book is the author's gift for presenting complex psychological models in a user-friendly style. Her techniques for self-awareness and reflection are accessible to any reader. If you are looking for love and confused by mixed messages, ghosting, and other weird cyber behaviors, *Committed: Finding Love and Loyalty Through the Seven Archetypes* can serve as a roadmap to finding a healthy relationship."

—Laurie Nadel, Ph.D. psychotherapist and bestselling author of *The Five Gifts: Discovering Hope, Healing and Strength When Disaster Strikes*

NEWMAN SPRINGS PUBLISHING
320 Broad Street
Red Bank, NJ 07701

First originally published by Newman Springs Publishing 2021

ISBN 978-1-63692-756-5 (Paperback)
ISBN 978-1-63881-258-6 (Hardcover)
ISBN 978-1-63692-757-2 (Digital)

Printed in the United States of America

Committed

FINDING LOVE AND LOYALTY THROUGH THE
SEVEN ARCHETYPES

CARMEN HARRA, Ph.D.
and
ALEXANDRA HARRA

We dedicate this book to you, dear reader,
who will have the love you deserve.

CONTENTS

INTRODUCTION

Commitment can't be forced, scheduled, or altered.
It either comes from the heart or it doesn't.
                                        —Carmen Harra

This is a book for people who seek commitment—the loyalty we all long for, the devotion for which we're genetically programmed. No one wants to be in an unstable relationship that crumbles at the slightest bit of turmoil, but not many of us are prepared to put in the never-ending effort it takes to uphold a relationship through time.

The goal of *Committed* is to help you achieve authentic, ardent love—the kind that fills you with excitement every morning and puts your mind at ease every night. That kind of commitment is, realistically speaking, hard to find and to keep.

A lot of people have trouble committing to another person because they're under the impression that they'll lose their power, independence, and personal satisfaction if they do so. This is far from true. Committing to the right partner will grant you even more fulfillment than you felt before. If you're experiencing problems in your relationship, it might be that you're trying to commit to the wrong person; dedicating yourself to someone who's unready or unwilling will bring you much more struggle than joy.

Committed is a relationship manual that will help you make the right choices in love by explaining the seven main archetypes you'll encounter, the promises they hold, as well as the challenges they pose to relationships. These archetypes are based on thirty years of counseling experience with tens of thousands of men and women.

While we agree that the human experience surpasses categories or formulas, it is also true that our character is formed and defined by our background.

Each of the seven archetypes we've identified has certain strengths and weaknesses in relationships, as well as fairly predictable patterns of behavior. By understanding each archetype and how he functions, you'll have a supportive framework for choosing a partner wisely, dealing with disputes as they arise, and making the most of your and your partner's strengths in creating a committed and lasting connection.

THE TROUBLE WITH COMMITMENT

Over half of all marriages end in divorce. Most people are aware of this scary statistic, yet they still get married! Many of them simply prefer to think, "That won't happen to me." Staying together for the long term is a dilemma for people across the globe, and some industries reap billions in profit from our commitment shortcomings. No one enters a relationship looking forward to the breakup, so why is it that so few of us can devote ourselves to another person? The answer to that is unique to each individual and can be a combination of mental, emotional, and physical factors. Through our work with so many female clients, we've come to believe that one main drawback is their lack of insight into basic male archetypes and how they respond to commitment issues. By exploring these seven personality types in detail, we'll walk you through the various reasons you might not be getting the love you deserve and teach you how to tackle the relationship challenges you're facing through the prism of archetypal understanding.

While we acknowledge that the notion of commitment varies from person to person, one of the keys to being in a strong, sound relationship is being able to distinguish between healthy and toxic kinds of love. This is easier said than done, as sometimes only a blurred line divides what's normal from what's not. Most people have never been taught how to make that distinction, which is why they repeatedly end up with partners that disappoint them or remain in relationships that are unsatisfactory. All too frequently, we hear statements like, "I'll never find a man to commit to me," and, "He's committed to me in his own way." Such beliefs are examples of ineffective and unhelpful approaches to commitment. But before you can change your approaches, you must first examine your outlook toward and insight into the nature of commitment.

Because commitment holds different meanings for different people, your definition is not the only correct one; as we'll demonstrate, genetics and upbringing, former experiences, the workings of the brain, and even ancestral karma all influence the way human beings love one another. In this book, we'll lead you to identify how you define commitment and, if needed, how to redefine it. You'll evaluate how you attend to your relationship needs, and, perhaps more importantly, you'll learn how to commit to yourself first.

Before you can love and commit to another person, you have to heal completely from whatever's happened in your past. You have to make sure you're ready and able to give the kind of commitment you want to receive, relinquishing all fear, doubt, and trauma, and taking responsibility for what you might've done wrong. If you're single, you need to be able to differentiate between a person who's serious and one who's still unsure, and remain vigilant for red flags (don't worry, we cover these too). If you're in a relationship, you need to be able to discern whether your significant other is truly capable of commitment (we believe almost everyone is) and maneuver around the roadblocks that have impeded you thus far.

Committed will guide you through these processes step-by-step. Our book first focuses on the inner work everyone needs to do, whether that person is ready for a relationship or not. We then shift to the framework of the seven archetypes that will help you, once you've completed your personal work, build a solid foundation for commitment with your current or prospective partner.

THE SEVEN ARCHETYPES

In our practice, we've identified seven main archetypes externalized in men and women: the Independent, the Workaholic, the Narcissist, the Free Spirit, the Hopeless Romantic, the Wounded Warrior, and the Introvert. We base our book around these archetypes because we've seen both genders embody each of them without fail. From our experience with countless clients over the past thirty years, we can tell you that many women who date a particular "type" of man don't know that such an archetype exists, let alone being able to diagnose the often-uncomfortable truths and tendencies of that archetype. They don't recognize with which archetype they're most and least compatible and don't understand how their relationship problems stem from their partner's persona.

For example, introversion is already a well-recognized personality style in psychology. There will be certain challenges in dating an Introvert that will be far different from dating, say, the Hopeless Romantic, who is psychologically obsessed with the notion of love. And there will be challenges of another order altogether if you're in love with a Narcissist, as selfishness seriously affects relationships.

The Workaholic is yet another prevalent archetype. We've worked with many female clients over the years whose relationships have collapsed because their partners were working long hours and not paying enough attention to them. An excessive preoccupation with work is a prime way to derail commitment. And yet it's possible to have a successful relationship with a Workaholic if you are of the right disposition and determination. This is true of every archetype you encounter. The key, once again, is assimilating the principal strengths and weaknesses of that archetype.

We strongly believe that every woman needs to fully comprehend the psychology of the archetype she's involved with so that she may help him break down relationship barriers and enable him to commit. Without understanding your loved one, you're flying without a map and more likely to crash. But by grasping the true nature of the seven archetypes, you expand your perception of commitment and find strategies for becoming, finding, and keeping a committed partner.

Once a person sheds self-imposed impediments and releases old beliefs, he or she becomes the Well-Rounded One, a loving ideal that's free of relationship burdens. *Committed* stands apart from other relationship books in that we provide a two-tier approach in helping you have a healthy and happy relationship not only with the archetype you're dating but also with yourself.

HOW *COMMITTED* CAN HELP YOU

Why are so many of us subconsciously afraid of commitment? What do we believe about it? What are our fears and hopes? Are these beliefs impairing us from love because they're outdated and misguided? We should not be rigid in our ideas or fixed in our ambitions. They require constant updating, like the software on a computer. As we pass through life and learn from trial and error, we have to revise our beliefs to make sure they're helping us move forward. If we find that they're keeping us in place or, worse, making us go backward, we must work to elevate them.

Chapters 1 through 4 will supply you with the tools to do the all-important work that each woman must perform on her own, no matter her past or current situation. Subconscious fears, psychological complexities, and inbred character flaws are some of the factors you'll have to address internally before you're ready for a committed relationship. You'll forsake the false, sometimes wild, and ultimately disappointing expectations that people often set up as standards for their love interests. Before you can find a devoted partner, you have to unlearn other people's versions of love and relearn your own.

After you reevaluate your commitment values, you'll have to practice them on yourself by committing to your needs each day. You'll be led through exercises that fortify your commitment to your health, career, family, and joy. You'll learn how to break through recurring relationship patterns that have kept you unhappy or alone.

For this reason, *Committed* will accompany you through the process of developing unshakable self-love so that you extend love to not just another partner but to the *right* partner. In the first few chapters of *Committed*, we'll usher you through the inner work you have to do in detail:

- Distinguish between what is always, what is sometimes, and what is never normal in a relationship.
- Hone your intuition so that you're instinctively guided toward a partner who can fulfill you and away from people who don't have genuine intentions.
- Successfully navigate the winding world of online dating.
- Revisit some less-than-favorite memories and make peace with them so as to detach from the past and step into the present.
- Adopt an entirely new definition of what it means to be flawed yet perfect in your own way.
- Learn how to enjoy your own company wholeheartedly before someone else enjoys it.
- Gently let go of people, places, and habits that no longer serve you, finally ending karmic cycles of unsuccessful relationships.
- Acknowledge your dominant emotion and learn to transmute it into a more constructive one rather than be controlled by it.

Committed then shifts its focus to the seven archetypes and the commitment issues and challenges that come with each. You'll learn how to tell the difference between a person who's ready to love, a person who's only in love with the idea of love, and a person who's deeply in love…with himself. The groundwork of the archetypes enables you to pair yourself with the best partner and to have a clear view of the work that lies ahead for you both. This second part of the book will help you:

- Identify the seven different archetypes and their basic qualities.
- Discover your own archetype.

- Understand the unique mindset, commitment capacity, and relationship inclinations of each archetype and how they relate to your own.
- Determine the challenges and benefits of being in a serious relationship with each archetype.
- Anticipate and address issues according to the needs, fears, desires, flaws, strengths, and weaknesses of each particular archetype.
- Recognize genuine compatibility and learn how to make the best commitment match based on the chemistry the archetypes share with each other.
- Create and maintain emotional intimacy.
- Receive real-world solutions to common and not-so-common relationship problems.

It's not enough to know why your significant other has trouble committing based on his archetype. We'll also show you how to make your partner commit, how to deepen his dedication to the relationship, and how to mediate external influences that cause distance and disconnection between you.

We firmly believe that no man is a commitment-phobe and almost anyone is capable of commitment. But there's a big "if" that follows: if he's willing to clear the obstacles that hinder his commitment abilities. Our objective, therefore, is to help you pinpoint the struggle between a man and his relationship, based on his particular archetype: what are the emotional and psychological components that must be resolved? Where is the blockage? Through the framework provided by the seven archetypes, you can resolve the internal and external conflicts that stand in the way of love.

You're meant to be with a person who shares your commitment goals and pushes you to become a better version of yourself each day. In its highest form, commitment is not a burden, responsibility, or a complication but a miracle.

Chapter 1

THE PSYCHOLOGY OF COMMITMENT

*Your beliefs are the pieces to your life puzzle. When
your beliefs change, the whole picture changes.*
—Carmen Harra

A CHANGING WORLD

A couple of years ago, I, Carmen, was in Romania getting ready to appear on a talk show. As I chatted backstage with the producer, I noticed a small group of young women standing off to the side, eyeing me hopefully. One of the members of the crew approached me and said, "They're fans of yours. They wanted to meet you." I smiled and waved the girls over, and they bounded up to me enthusiastically. I greeted the young women—who ranged in age between sixteen and twenty-five—and invited them to have a seat. They made no pretense about why they had come:

"Dr. Harra, Dr. Harra! Will I marry my boyfriend? His name's Christian," asked a redheaded girl who had reached me first.

"No, Dr. Harra, tell me first," interrupted her brunette friend. "Will I have a baby this year? My husband and I have been trying for so long!"

"Can you please tell me if the man I'm in love with loves me? Here—I brought his picture," piped up a third girl from the group.

I was happy to take turns answering the girls' questions but not entirely happy that they all shared the same content: each of these girls had come to inquire about their love lives, particularly when they would marry and have children. There was no mention of their personal ambitions.

As an intuitive psychologist, I'm used to answering tough questions on the spot. I get plenty of questions about love and relationships, of course. But I've noticed that young women in other countries are still more concerned about their relationships than other aspects of their lives. Here in America, we're taught to put ourselves first and believe that the rest will fall into place: get an education, build your career, work on yourself, and eventually you'll find the right person. But in many other parts of the world—specifically where religion remains a prominent force—a much heavier weight is placed on getting married and having a family, even in this day and age. Which of these approaches is right? It depends on whom you ask.

The idea of commitment is ingrained in our psyche through centuries of evolution. We've evolved from polygamous cavemen to monogamous couples forging lifetime ties. For thousands of years, we've been brought up to believe in commitment: every single culture and religion across the world promotes the loving alliance of two people. Commitment is taught as the most powerful bond available to humankind. It inspires integrity, totality, and wholeness, fulfilling our most basic need: the need to be loved. But its meaning has changed over time.

Commitment used to mean making a promise for life, unity under the eyes of God. Religion and societal roles were entwined into marriage, which was beheld as a sacrament. People would also commit to each other from an early age. Their goal in life was to find a partner, get married, and have a family. To offer an example from my own life, my mother married my father at twenty. My grandmother married my grandfather at sixteen—even younger! Though they never left each other, I sometimes wonder whether they really knew what love was at that age.

Possibly they grew to love each other in time. Possibly there were lesser grounds for severing ties with your other half. Usually, marriage was for life, so even if your partner cheated on you or abused you, you understood that you had no choice but to stay (especially if you were a woman). People knew how to stick together, yes, but it was partly because they had little to no other choice but to work through their differences.

Today, we have far more choices, as well as distractions and priorities. We can choose to cheat, separate from our partner, immerse ourselves in our careers, or surf the internet to forget our problems at home. More and more often in the Western world, we are choosing independence over commitment. But is this the right choice?

Women are expanding their roles in life: we are no longer just wives and mothers, cooks and caretakers. Modern women are career-driven powerhouses who are putting themselves first. We're taking back our historic power and fighting for equality. This is allowing us to embrace more assertive and goal-oriented roles like fast-paced entrepreneurs, small business owners, go-getters, visionaries, influencers, and innovators. This is wonderful and long overdue! But it also means that our reasons for partnering up are dwindling as other priorities take their place. We've developed an individualized mentality, removed from the whole and from our duties to community. Religion has also diminished in authority, taking the sanctity of marriage with it.

What impact is this self-attentive shift having on our love relationships? How are our beliefs and expectations evolving as a result? Is there a new commitment mentality emerging around the globe? We believe so.

The era of individuality is in full force. Everything from our smartphones to our living spaces to our (sometimes radical) hairstyles, tattoos, and clothing are tailored to fit our unique tastes. In regard to our relationships, we are placing greater emphasis on self-reliance and less on the need to receive care from another. Indeed, we are marching in the middle of a self-love movement. We're giving ourselves the love that our parents and grandparents used to get from a spouse.

This is not true for everyone, of course. Your version of commitment transforms as you advance through life. Maybe you felt hesitant about getting into a relationship, but then you met a person who showed you what a beautiful thing commitment can be. Or maybe you were yearning for a relationship, but you ended up with a man who vanquished that dream for you. Most men and women still crave commitment, but shifting attitudes about love have, at least to some degree, influenced everybody. This means it's harder than ever to find and keep a stable relationship.

Many people want to liberate themselves from the responsibility of commitment. Some of us now see commitment as having constricting, repressive connotations. Generations Y and Z have a notable problem with commitment. They may have witnessed their parents or family members struggling through their own relationships and they don't want to repeat that suffering.

Younger generations are also thoroughly turned off by divorce rates. As Alexandra says, "Why get married if your chances of getting divorced are greater than half? That's too much paperwork!" These statistics are discouraging to all of us, young or old, so we're practicing much greater care to whom we give our time and attention.

Social media might also be giving you enough attention so that you don't need it from a partner, but it's an empty sort of validation. Anyone can work their way up to thousands of likes if they put in enough effort (and wear limited articles of clothing), but keep in mind that the people behind those likes are complete strangers who can't do much for you except double-tap a photo. We must learn to differentiate attention that's authentic from attention that's artificial. Even achieving celebrity status pales in comparison to getting commitment from the person you love.

Online dating has made connecting with potential partners accessible and tempting. It's opened up a broad channel of virtual matchmaking with little or no rules; what you get out of online dating depends largely on what image you choose to portray. This modern method of finding love from the comfort of your own home, via a phone or laptop, has contributed greatly to the general shift in commitment. We offer our advice on online dating in chapter 2.

In a world that's changing so rapidly and unpredictably from one day to the next, it is key to probe into your beliefs and settle on ones that will propel you toward your unique commitment goals.

ASSUMPTIONS, ASSUMPTIONS

Each of us holds core beliefs about commitment to a long-term relationship, some of them contradictory. It either brings contentment or it's a prison. It's the most natural way of living or it goes against human nature. We hold such beliefs, but we don't evaluate why, how, or when they developed. Lifelong conditioning by our families, friends, the media, and popular culture has led to largely unexamined and often unrealistic views.

Many women come to us anxious before their wedding day. Why are they so nervous? They don't quite trust that they've found eternal devotion. They have the commitment they've always wanted, but they still have trouble believing it. It's not their partner that's the problem; it's the fact that they haven't secured their beliefs about love.

We're born having no notion of commitment. The definition of commitment is unique to each person and is shaped during childhood. It's first instilled in us by our parents and family members; what we witness at home forms the foundation for our life values, whether for good or ill. What we see at home we deem as "normal," though it may be far from normal. Kids imitate what they see, not what they're told. As we continue learning about the world around us, we start to digest the media's depiction of commitment: the way relationships are overly romanticized in movies and on TV awakens our primordial appetite for love. It also exposes the danger of pain and betrayal in relationships.

As you can imagine, this causes a broad range of commitment beliefs. Some men are entirely committed to one woman. Some men are with three women at once, and in their minds, there's nothing wrong with that. For other men, commitment simply entails paying the bills but not much else.

Children who come from whole families tend to create whole families for themselves when they grow up. Children who come from broken or turbulent homes may have a harder time finding and keeping commitment, although this is not always the case. This is partly because if there are emotional disruptions within the home, the child may not learn how to regulate his emotions and interact with others properly as he grows up. He is more likely to develop feelings of depression, anxiety, isolation, and loneliness, all emotions that will disturb his own personal relationships. We divulge more on this subject in chapter 3, as well as the reasons *why* we usually repeat what we see at home.

No matter what our backgrounds may be, whether we had a perfect childhood or struggled in a dysfunctional home, we all grow up with views of relationships that are distorted or unhealthy in some ways. We have to heal broken beliefs before we can create whole relationships.

Many women live with the false impression that they can change their partner. But how are we supposed to make other people acknowledge character complexes that they don't even realize they have? How can we bring to their awareness inner defects that they've spent their entire lives trying to hide? No one can change anyone else; we can only change ourselves. Other women speculate that pressure can get a man to commit. Pressure may make diamonds, but in a relationship, it only makes your partner resent you. Ultimatums ultimately end relationships; commitment must come from free will and free will alone. You also can't schedule commitment; everyone develops feelings and becomes dedicated at his or her own pace. No amount of convincing or begging can alter someone's feelings for you or make him commit before a deadline.

You should be intent on a fabulous future with your significant other without setting up expectations for him. Such expectations include your partner giving up his lifestyle and his friends for you or getting married and having a baby by a certain date. You're supposed to develop mutual goals and project the full potential of the relationship, but you're not supposed to impose your assumptions or presumptions upon the person you love. Don't force the hand of destiny or you risk ruining the beauty that could bloom between you. Commitment means recognizing your partner's unique capacity and working together to establish and improve a relationship you both believe in, but it doesn't mean pushing your personal beliefs and ambitions about commitment on each other. Continue working on yourself, encouraging your loved one to work on himself, and elevating the energy between you: journaling about the dreams you'd like to see coming true and visualizing the vacations you're going to take with your other half. Expect great things, but don't create expectations.

A big problem is that we don't examine our assumptions about commitment before getting involved with another person, and we don't take the time to find out what assumptions he holds. We sprint into a relationship knowing what movies we like or what food we prefer but understanding very little about what goes to the heart of bonding with another. If each of you is committed to yourself more than your partner, there won't be much of a relationship. But if each of you is aware of the other's patterns and perspective about commitment, there won't be any false expectations. Assumptions are constructs of our minds; they're things we'd like to be true or might be true. But we don't know which ones, if any, are actually true for our partner.

After getting married and having a child, Marcia simply stopped caring about her relationship. She gradually stopped tending to and communicating with her husband. In Marcia's mind, now that she was settled down, she didn't need to put in so much effort. We believe the cause for Marcia's change in behavior was twofold: she started getting used to her partner and giving all her attention to her child. It's not uncommon for one or both partners to "give up" on themselves as time goes by. Our dopamine levels drop as the years pass, and our lover no longer excites us like he used to. Realistically, parenting children also takes priority over everything else, including love relationships and one's own self-care.

Marcia's husband tried to convey that his needs weren't being met, although he continued to meet hers. Needless to say, Marcia was a bit surprised when she found out her husband was having an affair.

Commitment is unremitting work. "I do" is not a guarantee but a promise to do that work invariably.

If there's any secret to commitment, it's this: you must be with a person whose definition of devotion matches yours. It's okay if you're both Workaholics, as long as you're aware of how that might affect your dynamic. If you're both Introverts, you'll have a similar orientation to the social world. Whether you're both committed to raising children or helping the environment, you must be bound together by a shared passion.

Later in this chapter, we'll lead you through an exercise to help you identify your own attitudes about commitment.

FROM THE MIND TO THE REAL WORLD

Reality reflects what the mind projects.
—Carmen Harra

Thoughts are nothing short of magical; they are precursors to your reality. What you think is guaranteed to translate into reality because your mind is permanently linked to the divine. In that connection, you are all powerful, and no wish is denied to you. This is how the universe works: your thoughts create energy and that energy will attract or create similar energy. This is great if you have loving and compassionate thoughts, because you're more likely to bring in a loving and compassionate partner. But it's not so great if you carry around angry and insecure thoughts, as you'll find yourself in angry situations and draw in insecure people.

If you comprehend the link between thoughts, beliefs, and actions, you can rearrange your mental tapes and foster positive energy. Until you acknowledge which of your beliefs are harming you, you can't change them and change your reality in turn. Good relationships begin when we give up outdated assumptions. The reason you're not yet in the relationship you want, or why your relationships keep echoing old problems, is because of your belief system.

The first step to a committed and satisfying partnership is to fearlessly examine what you hold to be true.

WHAT BELIEFS DO YOU HOLD?

You can never go beyond your beliefs.
—Carmen Harra

We can never go beyond our beliefs, unless we change them first. Our beliefs shape our very reality. They paint the portrait of our world: everything we experience gets filtered through the lens of our beliefs first. This will cause problems if we're not grounded in the right beliefs or we're not grounded enough in our beliefs. We'll either hurt ourselves by adhering to destructive beliefs or alternate between different beliefs without being able to settle on one. Commitment is a belief system in and of itself, and we have to make sure we're following beliefs that support the relationships we strive to have.

In the haze of daily life, our beliefs can become obscured. Even our most firm beliefs can be tested as we become caught up in our minds, in our histories, and in our problems. We stop feeling the world in joyful or trusting ways. Frustration and impatience take the place of mindfulness. We become less aware, less intuitive, and less conscious of our intentions, thoughts, and actions. Our emotional intimacy with people fades away, and with it, our pleasure in living.

We know what it feels like to be in this state of affairs, but we don't spend much time reflecting on how we got to that point. We don't like to take much responsibility for the reality we created; many times we don't even want to admit that we're the ones who create our reality, placing the blame on bad luck or other people instead. In order to live full and vibrant lives, it's vital that we understand what impact our beliefs have on the quality of our lives on a moment-by-moment basis.

The following questions will help you begin to identify deeply embedded beliefs that influence the way you experience relationships and commitment. Awareness of your beliefs is the start of breaking away from assumptions that hold you back.

1. What thoughts do you keep thinking? Your brain is programmed by your habits (we'll explain this more in following chapters). Ever notice that the more you think about something, the harder it is to get your mind off it? That's because the neurons in your brain form clusters around your thoughts. Because of increased traffic on those neural pathways, you'll continue to think those same thoughts. Obsessive thinking creates anxiety, which turns into depression, which feeds more obsessive thoughts. Like a broken record, the same thoughts cause you to simulate the same actions (often not very positive ones). If your thoughts tend toward fear, hatred, or vindictiveness, you're caught in an unhappy cycle. But most of us aren't even aware of what we're thinking about most and how that thought affects our mood and outlook on life.

Exercise: To find out what you routinely think, we want you to keep track of your thoughts for the course of one or two days. You can do this by jotting down notes in your phone or in a small notebook as the day progresses. They can be short entries, a line or two whenever a strong thought comes up, like "Expecting an argument with Ted today" or "Worried about the political situation" or "Thrilled to see spring coming." Don't judge or censor what you write down.

After a day or two of jotting down your thoughts, inspect your thought diary. Do you see certain thought sequences? Are you surprised by how repetitive they are? Are your thoughts more negative than positive? Which emotion pops up most frequently in your thoughts? Bitterness? Envy? Regret about the past? Fear of the future? Or is it joy, ambition, and a sense of fulfillment?

An old saying goes like this: what you fear, you attract. We have a slightly different view: what you obsess over, you tend to notice more and more, until that's almost *all* you notice! If you're afraid of bugs, you won't start attracting more bugs. Rather, your obsession will make you see bugs everywhere. More alert to their presence, you may be the first to notice a spider when others do not.

If you're obsessed with finding commitment, you'll brood over this thought until it takes over your life. Whenever you watch a romantic movie, you'll think that all your friends are in great relationships except you. You may become so obsessed that you'll commit to someone who's not the right choice, just for the sake of being able to say you have a partner. When the honeymoon ends, however, the same old problems will transpire and the cycle will repeat.

Fear is your worst enemy in a relationship. Overactive and fearful thoughts lead you to make hasty and desperate decisions that lead to unhappy consequences. Anger, fear, or any emotion, for that matter, will manifest itself eventually. It's imperative that you become aware of what you're thinking and tame counterproductive thoughts.

Sound impossible? It isn't! You can shift the content and course of your thoughts simply by paying attention. The key is to allow negative thoughts to come and go like visitors: welcome them, get to know them, then show them the door. When a recurring thought pops up, don't indulge it. If you find yourself having fear-inducing thoughts, replace them with more accepting thoughts. You hold full control over your mind.

Your mind immediately defaults to the worst possible outcome as a way of defending you from shock or trauma. It prepares you for the worst so that if the worst does happen, it won't seem so bad. But this sort of thinking actually exacerbates the situation in the real world. If you're assuming a negative outcome about something, why not imagine a positive outcome instead? Visualize a different scenario, one that's more favorable to you. There's no need to think about the things you fear because they haven't yet happened and don't need to happen.

Practice this exercise on a daily basis. In time, your neurons will link around the more positive thoughts and you'll find your mind becoming a much brighter place.

2. To whom are you listening? How do you make decisions? Are you influenced by what other people say and do or do you heed the voice of your intuition?

If you have a strong sense of self, you won't have to look outside yourself for guidance. Finding yourself is miraculous: it's a genesis of your own truth. You'll think twice before following what everyone else is saying and doing because superior guidance will radiate from within.

Exercise: When making decisions, or when evaluating your life, who influences you? Whose standards or ideas are you judging yourself by—are they your mother's, your boyfriend's, your friends', or your own? Are those standards and ideas realistic? Write down your responses. What have you learned? Did anything surprise you?

3. *What is your first reaction?* Difficult moments reveal who we are in vivid and sometimes unflattering ways. What is your first reaction to an unpleasant situation? Do you become irritated and angry? Respond with calm and patience? Do you run away if you encounter difficulty? Or do you try to resolve the problem thoughtfully?

Exercise: Record your reaction to minor aggravations over the next few days: a traffic jam, a long line at the supermarket, an argument, or a frustrating workplace or household task. When you're done, notice what your typical reaction was. Annoyance? Understanding? Calm? Nervousness?

Your initial reaction to minor inconveniences is usually your reaction to life in general. If you keep your composure in moments of stress, you're probably a calm person most of the time. If you're truculent and aggressive, then you're probably angry much of the time. This can be an unpleasant insight to face, but accepting the problem and the way you react to it are catalysts for your personal growth.

If anger is the first thing you feel, try changing your reaction to small problems as they crop up during the day. Try responding with acceptance instead. This takes practice, and we'll give you more instructions on transmuting emotions in chapter 4. Have faith that you'll learn to skip over the destructive emotions and reach a resolution more quickly. Negative emotions do nothing to help you find a solution anyway. As you change your reaction to small things, you'll develop a greater ability not to overreact to big things.

4. How do you regard others? As you weave your way throughout your day, notice your attitude toward others. Are you disappointed in humanity? Easily spot other people's flaws? Do you avoid making eye contact or striking up a friendly conversation? Or do you genuinely like other people? Do you believe in their general goodness? The way you regard others reveals what's going on inside you.

Exercise: Keep a log of your reactions to people during the course of a day, whether it's someone on the phone, a friend or family member, your coworkers, or interacting with strangers in a public space.

What did you learn about your reactions? What feelings do you harbor toward others? Fear? Insecurity? Openness? Judgment? A sense of trust?

Seeing people in a mostly negative light means you've been hurt and disappointed, and it's time to heal. If you're shut within yourself, it's time to gently open up to others. If your first thought or reaction is negative, try changing it. We're all struggling through something, but we should be simultaneously working to surpass it.

We know that it's easy to lose trust in people. Some of us got bad deals in childhood. Many of us have been let down by others more than once. A failed relationship may open wounds you thought were closed for good. But you must never lose faith that there are many kindhearted, like-minded folks out there. Becoming cynical about humanity will lead nowhere, and it certainly won't create the kind of energy that will lead the right person to you.

If you find yourself suddenly frustrated or irritated, or lashing out at innocent people around you, stop and ask yourself: "What was I just thinking about that caused these emotions to surface?" Investigate your feelings, for in them you will find your answers.

The only two things you need to reshape your life are awareness and desire. Let these exercises awaken a greater awareness of your beliefs and a burning desire to change those beliefs for the better.

FALSE EXPECTATIONS IN RELATIONSHIPS

Before we can begin to define what commitment is, we must define what it *isn't* by unlearning assumptions that limit our potential to be in a loving relationship. As with anything else in life, commitment comes with limitations. All relationships are finite in one way or another. No one will ever be able to give you complete bliss because no one, including you, is perfect (we know you come close to it though!). And that's okay, because the magic of relationships comes from working through your imperfections together. But that can't happen unless you relinquish false expectations and view relationships realistically.

Here are the most common false expectations we hear all too frequently:

"We'll always have fireworks. Our chemistry and romance will keep us together."

Chemistry and romance come and go. The excitement of sex wears off. You see your partner every day and the monotony sets in. Your opinions and views of the world may split in opposite directions over time. This may sound like a negative scenario, but it's a reality for all long-term relationships.

"He'll provide for me."

He might, up to a certain point. But what will you do if your partner is your only source of money and something happens to him one day? A man is never a financial plan.

"They're just a few bad habits."

You must be able to distinguish between innocent offenses and serious red flags for the sake of your well-being. Forgetting to put the toilet seat down is a bad habit. Lying pathologically is a red flag.

"I can change him."

As we said before, no one can change a man but himself. To change, he must have a desire to improve his current behavior.

"Giving him a child will make our relationship better," or, *"A child will make him commit."*

It may, or it may make things worse and forever tie you to a person who's not right for you. Not even ten children can make an unwilling partner commit! Having a child is a blessing, but having a child with the *right* partner is the biggest blessing.

"It has to come from him."

Wait for him to call and you might be waiting forever. Sometimes you have to put your pride aside and make the first move. The bottom line is that it has to come from both of you.

"I don't need to change anything about myself."

You're human, which already means you're imperfect. Just as your partner has personality traits you dislike, so do you have traits he dislikes. You should try to become a better person each day—not for your partner but for yourself.

"He has an obligation to me."

Once you're an adult, no one has an obligation to you. Not even in marriage does your spouse have to give you everything you want. The only person who has an obligation to you is you!

"If I complain, I'll get what I want."

You might, but constantly complaining might also cause some big damage to your relationship. You must stand your ground, but never whine about every little thing.

"The past won't interfere."

Unless you've closed all the doors to your past (and locked them and thrown away the key), the past will very much become your present and future. You must understand how your karma works if you want to understand why certain things are happening and how to prevent them from happening again.

"That would never happen to me."

This is what we all like to think: I'll never get sick, I'll never lose my money, I'll never get cheated on, and other unfortunate things that end up happening to everyone sooner or later. While you shouldn't live life worrying that something bad will happen, you should be prepared for anything. In relationships, always expect the unexpected.

"Who cares about a stupid football game?"

It's a misconception that men don't need pampering or that they don't require as much attention, care, and gentleness as a woman. Respect your partner's hobbies, whether they're watching football games or tinkering with cars or collecting comic books.

"I know I'm in a compromise, but at least he gives me money for the kids."

This should never be the price you put on love. You'll grow weary of compromising your values and happiness in time. Providing financial stability cannot compare to providing emotional stability.

"If I make him jealous, he'll want me."

Purposely doing things to make a man jealous will only do one thing: hurt the relationship. Your partner should be made aware that you'll leave if he doesn't treat you right, but there are better ways of making him realize this than invoking his envy.

"I can replace him."

You can replace your car if it gets damaged or your purse if it gets stolen, but you can't replace a human being. You may think that a new boyfriend will be better than your ex-boyfriend, but this will prove false: a new partner won't be better; he'll only be different. You may be more compatible, but he'll still have some qualities you like and others you dislike. No one is better or worse than anyone else; we just are.

"Something is better than nothing."

Depending on the circumstances, nothing is sometimes much better than something—especially if that "something" is a person who's causing you pain and confusion. Some women have gotten used to hearing from their significant other once a week or seeing him once a month. Having only something, only a fraction of a real partner, is like having only one piece of the whole: you will constantly feel like something is missing.

"He has to be tall, dark, and handsome...oh, and rich."

The only place you'll find Prince Charming is in a children's book. The man who will make you happiest will be riddled with problems, some of which are temporary and some of which are permanent. Let go of the notion that you'll meet a perfect, flawless man, as this will lead to unending disappointment.

If you hold any of these assumptions, it would benefit your relationship to reevaluate your beliefs.

IDENTIFYING YOUR OWN MISCONCEPTIONS

Reflect on the list you just read. Choose three main misconceptions that most apply to you and contemplate them for a moment. Then feel free to jot down your answers below:

Where do these misconceptions come from?

_____.

What problems might they pose in a future relationship?

_____.

What problems have they already created in my past relationships?

_____.

How can I reduce such assumptions?

_____.

If I reduced these misconceptions, my relationship would improve in these ways:

_____.

If you want to add to or adjust this exercise, please do, as long as it helps you identify erroneous beliefs.

EXPLORING PSYCHOLOGICAL BARRIERS TO COMMITMENT

Commitment begins as a state of mind; devotion is the result of mental readiness. Sometimes, however, we're ready to commit when the other person is not. When we realize this, we think, *Why isn't he ready? Why is this happening again? Was it me?* The answer is no, it's not you, but your partner may have psychological barriers that need to be broken down.

Diana married her husband, Daniel, at a very young age. She simply couldn't resist what he had to offer: Daniel had money. Diana came from a lower-class family and saw this man as her escape from financial struggles. But she had not yet made the distinction between falling in love with *a person* and falling in love with *the idea* of a person. She ignored the red flags, gave up on her education, and moved in with Daniel. Time unveiled that Daniel was bipolar. At times, he was sweet and loving. At other times, some trigger switched on his rage and he beat Diana and called her every name in the book.

Diana's biggest mistake was not divorcing earlier on. She believed she could change Daniel or at least help him in some way. Diana was so focused on making Daniel happy that she forgot what made her happy. She was so adamant about Daniel's well-being that she made herself unwell. Diana learned the hard way that she should have become independent, self-loving, and strong on her own before seeking a relationship.

A relationship becomes onerous when one or both partners haven't addressed their psychological complexities. Love can paralyze logic, which makes things worse because we tend to stop thinking when we start feeling. An unsuccessful relationship can peel away our protective layers, leaving us fragile and vulnerable. Things we thought would never happen to us again, happen to us again. Emotions we thought we had dealt with erupt with a fury. We find ourselves in the same arguments and impasses.

UNDERSTANDING YOUR PARTNER'S CORE BELIEFS

Regardless of his archetype, your partner has to possess certain values that help a relationship survive and thrive in time. Before you can begin to dissect a man's love personality, you have to glean the core beliefs he holds about life. Because if his virtues are weak, wrong, or backward, your relationship (and you) will be affected. Pondering these questions and considering how your partner would act in such scenarios will provide you key insight into his belief system:

What does your future look like? Can you imagine building together? Can you envision yourself growing old with this person? If your partner shows serious flaws—like addiction, abuse, or pathological lying—you may not be able to see a future by his side. Visualize your relationship in five, ten, or even twenty years down the road. How do you expect it to change? More importantly, how do you expect it to evolve?

How does he regard family? Does he have close ties with his family members? Is family a priority? Even if your partner has experienced familial rifts (which can happen to anyone), has he cared enough to try to work things out? You should be sympathetic to your partner's relationship with his family—whatever that relationship might be—but you also have to anticipate that the way he treats his family is the way he will treat you when you become a member of his household. Remember also that the same family issues (like if he hates his mother or doesn't see his kids) are likely to play out again if you decide to have a family with this person. Be mindful of your partner's family karma and how this might affect you one day.

Can he compromise? Compromise is the almighty answer to a lasting relationship. Do you and your partner believe in compromise over being right? Is he willing to give and take with you on essential matters? A relationship without compromise is a road with a dead end.

Does he share your mentality? Even if you come from different backgrounds, you and your partner should have a similar mindset.

Are your views on life in sync? Are your morals complementary? Sharing concurrent goals is more likely to keep you together.

What emotions does he trigger? The greatest gift anyone can give you is peace of mind. You should not be in a relationship with a man who evokes anxiety, worry, or fear all the time; if he does, it means he hasn't developed enough integrity and consideration for others. A partner who inspires tranquility and steadies the emotions within you is like water to a rose garden: he will help you flourish into your most incredible self.

How does he compare to other partners? Have you brought into your life someone who's a lot like a former partner? Or does he hold positive qualities that previous partners lacked? If you didn't completely heal from and resolve your karma, you might attract a person who's a near copy of your ex (we'll teach you how to break this cycle in chapter 3). Compare patterns that existed in past relationships with things that are happening in your current relationship to ensure you're making progress.

Can you tolerate each other's weaknesses? Having the right commitment beliefs will grant you a certain degree of tolerance. Can you and your partner "stand" all of each other's faults? Do you appreciate each other's way of being? Unconditional love calls that we accept our partner's weaknesses in the same way as his strengths.

Do you see potential for improvement? Human beings are highly prone to error. The fact is that you'll never find a perfect partner; every person who walks through your life will leave flawed footprints. We all need a bit of work, and we all have one vice to which we keep reverting. This can be anything from gambling to careless spending. You'll have to detect your partner's bad habit from early on and decide whether you'll be able to put up with it for the long term, because it may or may not improve with time. Constructive beliefs increase a person's ability to change for the better.

What has he taught you? The right partner will double as your teacher. Two souls that vibrate on the same level will have much to learn from one another. Whether they're lessons in love, work, finances, forgiveness, or any other element of life, your partner should motivate you to expand mentally and evolve spiritually.

What are his priorities? Your partner's priority should be you. We understand this can't always be the case, as your partner also has a career, family, and other obligations to attend to. Evaluate how he prioritizes his responsibilities and in which place you fall among them. If you put your partner first, you should also be first on his list. If you feel like you're not, it's time to rearrange your own list of priorities. Under no circumstances should you be with a person who prioritizes drinking, hanging out with the wrong people, or other such behaviors over you.

Deliberating the answers to these questions will reveal your partner's core beliefs. And if you're unhappy with some of the answers, you should think about whether your partner is giving off red flags that shouldn't be ignored.

Chapter 2

(AB)NORMAL RELATIONSHIPS

What we keep experiencing, we keep expecting.
—Alexandra Harra

What is a normal relationship? What's an abnormal one? Who determines these things? You'll receive different answers from every woman you ask: the one who's been lied to and cheated on might tell you that "All men are the same." The wife who's been married to her wonderful husband of thirty years might say "Unconditional love and support." Normality is subject to personal experience, but if our relationships aren't the healthiest, our interpretation of love can become distorted. Whatever your definition may be, we can all agree on is this: a normal relationship is one in which both partners help, encourage, and rely on each other. A balanced relationship stimulates our highest feelings: love, acceptance, and empathy.

One word we've been hearing a lot lately is "toxic." Toxic refers to something that is poisonous and harmful. In terms of love, a toxic relationship is one that causes more harm than good and creates frequent feelings of anxiety, anger, and even desperation. But are toxic relationships becoming the new norm? Because we become immune to everything we experience, we can easily mistake our own toxic relationships for normal ones. For this reason, you have to honestly evaluate the things that are happening between you and your partner and face the reality of your relationship. The first person who will tell you that your relationship (or a part of it) is toxic will be yourself. Your own intuition will reveal whether you should be involved with a person or not. Always trust your gut, no matter how far it seems from the reality of the moment; when something *seems* off, it *is* off. People know how to lie, but your intuition doesn't. Also rely on your inner voice to assure you that it's safe to growth with, learn from, and be with a person for many years to come. Normal relationships are fair and balanced with both partners putting in the necessary amount of effort. One side shouldn't be doing more than the other.

Your relationship should not be marked by unending arguments, yelling, bickering, temper tantrums, or any form of violence. No matter how much you both swear you love each other and want to be together, unless these kinds of emotions are controlled, the relationship isn't healthy for either person involved. The energy between you should be as placid as the surface of a lake. Everyone becomes angry once in a while, and that's tolerable. As long as your relationship doesn't involve daily outbursts of anger, there's no reason why it can't move forward.

But if your partner is repeatedly lying to you about where he's going, who he's seeing, and what he's doing, the relationship can't get too far. Pathological liars are characterized by serial dishonesty. To them, a lie is simply easier to tell than the truth. Everyone will get caught telling a little white lie here and there, but your partner shouldn't be deceiving you regularly. Integrity and honesty should be alive, and both of you should be trusting each other's words as the truth. A healthy relationship won't have you feeling uncomfortable about any part of yourself or increase your insecurities. Your partner should point out your strongest traits and encourage you to become even better.

Any form of addiction in a relationship is abnormal. It is extremely cumbersome to live with an alcoholic, drug user, or a person who suffers from a mental or emotional disorder. In the long run, these types of behavioral issues will take their toll on both partners, hurting not only the person who has the condition but the person who cares for him. Both partners must have a pure mind, body, and soul, and recognize the importance of physical, emotional, and mental health.

You must match each other on a mental level too. Your partner is supposed stir up your mental senses with his knowledge and wisdom. This means that he should continually engage you, intrigue you, and stimulate you. Relationships have to be alive on a mental note just as much as in the physical sense. If your love interest doesn't provoke your mind, you probably aren't compatible.

Lastly, it's not normal if you no longer feel love for the person you're with. You might stay with him for the sake of not splitting up (for the children or financial stability), but if love is absent, you'll have a persistent, nagging feeling that something is missing. You should still be able to count the reasons why you fell in love with your partner, and your feelings for him should remain consistent over time.

RECOGNIZING RED FLAGS

Red flags usually appear early on and indicate unhealthy behaviors. You have to learn to read these flags—some obvious, some subtle—as soon as they reveal themselves to avoid falling into an abnormal relationship.

Pay close attention to discrepancies that cause you to question your partner's intentions, words, and actions. Refrain from making excuses for him. Be honest with yourself and acknowledge when your partner isn't acting in good faith or isn't making you happy. Impulses that seem insignificant can be early indicators of greater issues that will escalate in time. As you'll see, an annoying quirk is not the same thing as a red flag.

Reconsider your commitment to a person who's complicated, because if it's complicated from the beginning, it will only become more complicated in time. Everyone carries a bit of baggage, including you. That's normal. What's not normal is a person who hauls entire loads from their past into your present life. Your partner may have children from a previous relationship, but his kids shouldn't make your life miserable. Your partner may have trust issues from bad experiences, but his trust issues shouldn't force you to prove your every move. If a relationship starts off this burdensome, it will only require more effort with each passing day. Release it from your life and find a love that's lighthearted and joyful.

Compromise can save a relationship from complications. But if a person refuses to compromise, the relationship can't survive. A person's inability to compromise quickly becomes evident. Your partner should be offering compromise freely, and you should be taking turns giving in to each other. If he doesn't, the relationship will entail much sacrifice on your part.

Equal to compromise is emotional stability. Steer clear of the person who displays mood swings because this will disrupt your inner harmony. Your partner shouldn't leave you exhausted by the end of the day! If you're exposed to anger, bitterness, or resentment all the time, you might find yourself duplicating these emotions and becoming a person you don't want to be. Riding an emotional roller coaster will take a mental and physical toll on you. If your partner shifts from delighted to depressed in seconds, understand that a psychological imbalance exists. And if he gets angry over everything, know that his anger will eventually spill onto you.

If your partner isn't emotionally stable, he most likely isn't generous either. Generosity takes many forms, the most obvious being monetary. A person must also be giving with his time, affection, advice, and good intentions. Such rewards are invaluable. Stinginess and greediness are serious red flags. While you shouldn't expect to receive the world on a silver platter, you deserve a partner who's fair and gives back as much as he takes. Your partner should immediately offer help when you're in need. Generosity is rare, so be grateful for the partner who is giving in all senses of the word. The person who wants to share his world with you is preparing for a future with you.

This holds true as long as he's sharing with you, and not with multiple women! If you discover your partner being disloyal, spare yourself the heartbreak and move along. Chances are that he was prone to infidelity long before he met you and will continue to be this way throughout your relationship. We hope we can make people better or mold their characters, or that they will somehow be different with us than they were in past relationships. This sort of thinking leads us into a pit of disappointment as we realize that people will continue being who they are until they decide to change themselves.

Be careful about becoming too attached to the person who treats others poorly, like talking down to people, being rude without reason, or being mean to his family members. People who have problems with themselves often take it out on those closest to them. Your partner may treat you nicely in the beginning, but the same issues he has with other people in his life will creep into your own relationship down the line.

It's demoralizing when the person you like doesn't check in with you or send a simple text. One of the most frequent complaints we hear from our clients is that their partner doesn't initiate conversation; they have to be the ones to send the first message or make the call. Even worse is when he disappears then reappears days later like nothing happened. Beware of settling with a person who's emotionally distant. You'll find yourself telling him the same thing over and over again, which will go in one ear and come out the other.

Your partner should be able to take care of himself. The way in which someone treats (or mistreats) himself is reflective of the way he will treat you. If your partner is self-destructive, how can he strengthen you? If he's completely careless with his home, job, belongings, health, finances, or appearance, chances are he won't be able to lend you the care you need and deserve. Look for someone who handles himself responsibly, lovingly, and gently so that he can treat you in this same manner.

Last but not least, consider your partner's dating history. Has he been able to sustain at least one serious relationship? It'll be difficult for him to keep up long-term love if he's used to jumping from romance to romance. You should be with a person who not only wants to fortify a relationship with you through time but who understands the hard work needed to do so. A partner who expresses the desire for commitment *and* redoubles his words with actions is a real treasure.

Our impulses predict our true nature. Put your well-being first and beware of engaging in a serious relationship with a person who shows such tendencies. Keep these red flags in mind as we explore the dos and don'ts of online and in-person dating and the phenomenon known as ghosting next.

THE MAN BEHIND THE PROFILE

Many women find men through online dating, which saves them time and possibly a couple of cringe-worthy dates. They recount their stories to us: some are positive, some negative, and others just plain bizarre. Here, we outline ways that women can safely date online and circumvent finding and falling for men who won't commit. We know that online dating can be a confusing and intimidating world of its own! But there are also plenty of men behind the profile seeking the same level of devotion as you.

Dating via the internet is a new and tempting invention of the modern world. In the old world, arranged marriages were widespread; people had little choice in what partner was picked for them, which seems like a pretty depressing drawback. But there were a few pros too: at least the bride's parents knew her husband-to-be's family. There were also greater expectations of the husband back then, like providing for his family and sticking with his wife through thick and thin. Back in those days, you would wed a person from your own city or town. Unless you were a member of a royal family, there was little chance of marrying a person who lived halfway across the globe. This made the notion of commitment more predictable overall.

Online dating can feel like walking into a jungle: you don't know what sorts of creatures you'll encounter. In October 2019, the Pew Research Center surveyed 4,860 US adults about their online dating experiences. A larger number of younger women reported having troublesome interactions on online dating platforms. This leads us to believe that many men who create an online dating profile do so for entertainment; they want to see what, if anything, can come out of it. The website represents that

Six-in-ten female users ages 18 to 34 say someone on a dating site or app continued to

contact them after they said they were not interested, while 57% report that another user has
sent them a sexually explicit message or image
they didn't ask for. At the same time, 44% report
that someone called them an offense name on a
dating site or app, while 19% say they have had
someone threaten to physically harm them.

These are alarming statistics, but the truth of the matter is that in-person dating presents equal dangers.

While you do run a risk of meeting the wrong person online, it's a useful dating tool in the right hands, not to mention that it's the inarguable future of dating; online dating will take over in preference to in-person dating. According to eHarmony, there are over forty million Americans using online dating. Of young adults, 27 percent report using such sites, which is up from 10 percent in 2013. There are also slightly more men than women using online dating. One obvious problem is that you don't know who's behind the picture-perfect profile and if he's divulging his true intentions. eHarmony reports that 53 percent of people lie on their online dating profile about things like their age, income, and height/weight. Personally, we believe the percentage is higher. And if you start dating online, don't be surprised if you break up online too. You're likely to break up by email—and we thought a breakup text was bad!

Virtual dating can broaden your possibilities, but you can also get lost in having too many possibilities. We've had clients tell us that online dating felt like looking for a needle in a haystack. We understand their concerns; how do you find your best match amid thousands of candidates? Having so many choices may or may not a good thing. It can be counterproductive to commitment if you feel like you have too many options and can't focus on one. It can also feel like it interferes in the course of your destiny and the people you're fated to meet.

Our client Maggie divorced her husband after three kids and many years of marriage. As a typical Workaholic, her husband didn't pay much attention to her throughout their marriage. After her divorce, it was only normal that Maggie was excited to start dating and get the love of which she had been deprived for so long. Maggie set up an account and, being a good-looking woman, suitors flocked to her profile. She went on a myriad of dates, but she noticed that they were with men who didn't want commitment, only amusement. Maggie wanted to have fun too, but two years into it, she realized that her multitudinous dates weren't getting her anywhere: she was no closer to finding a committed relationship than she had been on the day her divorce was finalized. On the contrary, she felt disappointed in her online escapades.

In cases like this, online dating can work against commitment if you get caught up in the idea of talking and flirting with many people at once. You can have multiple dates, multiple partners—in multiple cities if you want! It can be a lot of fun but doesn't necessarily promote the notion of commitment. If you don't remain focused, online dating can subtract from the value of investing in one person and lead to the idea of investing in a lot of people. When Maggie did find a real relationship, it was through one her friends who introduced her to a kind and handsome man named Bruce (who had no online profiles).

A more positive instance of online dating was Jordana, who found her husband of (now) twelve years on an online dating site. Jacob was younger than Jordana, so she was hesitant to give in to his attempts to take her out. But when the two finally met, they instantly clicked and became inseparable.

After I, Carmen, lost my late husband, I was offered the rare opportunity to join an exclusive matchmaking club...for a mere $7,000. I considered that the money was better donated to charity than spent on matchmaking services. Neither Alexandra nor I are much in favor of spending money to find love; you could spend a small fortune to be matched with your soul mate, but if it's not meant to happen that way, no amount of money in the world will bring him to you. On the other hand, when your fates are aligned, you could be taking out the garbage in house slippers and bump into a man who ignites all your senses at once.

Before you begin scouring through photos of singles, you have to make sure you're putting yourself out there in the best light possible to attract a stable and well-intentioned man. The golden rule in dating is that you will receive the energy you put out. This means assessing how you're portraying yourself to potential partners: what kind of photos are you uploading? Do you consider them conservative or risqué? What language are you using? Is it straightforward or playful? What are the first things you disclose about yourself? Psychologically speaking, these are usually the things you're most proud of! For example, it's one thing to fill your "about" section with your postgraduate degrees and another to list your features in *Playboy*. There are many sides to every woman, and there is no right or wrong way to be; it all depends on what you want to attract.

This applies to in-person dating as well. Whether a handsome stranger at your gym asked you out or you're ready to come face-to-face with the guy who's been filling up your inbox, your first dates are the most important to create excitement and attraction between you. When you do get to sit down and engage in conversation with a person you like, you'll have to ask strategic questions that reveal his innermost essence. You may be curious to find out what his favorite pizza topping is, but such details are trivial in the greater scheme of things. Try to stick to subjects that relate to his challenges and aspirations. Great questions to ask are, "What does the ideal relationship look like to you?" and, "Where do you see yourself in five years?"

When it comes time to answer questions about yourself, it's okay to be frank. You can admit to him why your former relationship failed, especially if it's done with the intention of avoiding such problems in the future. If your ex spent too much time apart from you, make sure to emphasize that spending time together is important to you. Or if your last partner put no effort into the relationship, you should make it clear that you're only willing to be in a relationship in which both partners put in equal amounts of work. Being sincere from the beginning helps avoid mistakes that were made in former relationships. It will save you much time if you come to the conclusion that this person doesn't hold the same values as you.

Another topic you should bring up on your first few outings together are the lessons you've learned about love. Share what your past relationships have taught you about human nature, patience, communication, etc. In this way, you show that you've evolved from relationship to relationship. You also get to find out what your date has learned from his romantic endeavors. You're allowed to divulge what caused you to feel dissatisfied, like the lying, cheating, or whatever else disappointed you in past relationships. Confess, too, your own former faults, like if you were too needy, judgmental, or insecure. If your date is the right person for you, he'll bear these details in mind and avoid such behavior.

What you shouldn't admit—at least not right away—is how much you loved your ex, even if you think it's safe to do so because you no longer care about him in the present. Every love relationship you encounter will be completely different, but *none* will be perfect because no human being is perfect. Even your soul mate will lack some elements. There's no comparing the degrees of love you felt for various partners, so leave out the "strong feelings" you used to have for your ex. And if you can't help but compare and contrast your date and your ex, at least do it in your mind.

These include explanations of your and your ex's sex life. Unless it weirdly excites your date, don't delve into sexual details from your past, like what your ex physically did and did not do to and for you. It will make your potential partner feel like he has to live up to your ex's intimate standards. Build the foundation of your physical relationship little by little, suggesting to him what you like and giving what he likes in turn.

Then there are some things you should not give away until you thoroughly know the person, and even things you need never tell your loved one, not even if he becomes your spouse. The most important of these are family secrets. What happened in your family should, out of respect, remain in your family.

When you're ready to visit a new partner's home for the first time, allow yourself to be led by your intuition. Take mental notes of your initial impressions about his intimate space. Pay attention to the energy of it; the way someone lives reveals a lot about him! If his place is super messy, he could be a careless person. If it's a bit too tidy, he might be hiding something or trying to make up for something he thinks he lacks inside. If it's overly cluttered, it's possible he's holding onto the past. Or if things are broken or missing, he may be a procrastinator. When you leave, jot down your thoughts. Read over what you wrote a few months later, after you get to know the person, and you'll be surprised to find how right you were.

Online dating can be a highly useful tool in finding a relationship, but it should not be your only resource. Explore your options and don't limit yourself to one means of meeting the right person for you. Be selective about whom you give your time to and agree to meet only users with whom you feel strongly connected. Remember that the majority of users on dating sites are just browsing. You don't need an inbox full of false promises; a single sweet message from the right person is enough. You don't have to go on a dozen dates to feel good; one night out with an amazing person will suffice. You can come to know a person online up to a certain point, but true connections are always forged face-to-face. We encourage you to practice common sense and apply the principle of quality over quantity when it comes to any kind of dating.

MEN WHO GHOST

Whether you met online or in person, ghosting is equally painful. Ghosting means cutting off communication with a love interest without offering an explanation. Ghosting hurts because it demolishes our hope; we think we've finally found love only to be let down again. We shouldn't have to approach love half-heartedly, afraid that a person will dissolve into thin air if we like him too much or open up too soon. It's natural to feel uncurbed enthusiasm and to envision a future with a potentially great partner. What are you supposed to do, then, when he suddenly goes missing for days or doesn't reach out for weeks?

Ghosting is more common now than ever. In 2018, the *Journal of Social and Personal Relationships* surveyed 1,300 people. Of the participants, one-quarter answered that they had been ghosted by a partner and one-fifth admitted to having ghosted someone themselves. Chances are that this has happened to you: a man who at first appears intensely interested vanishes faster than Houdini in his final act. You may have gathered from what you read that certain archetypes, namely the Independent and Free Spirit, are more inclined to drop the woman they're talking to abruptly. While any of the archetypes can be guilty of ghosting, the Independent fears the implications of commitment and the Free Spirit can't settle on one thing. While this doesn't excuse the actions of a ghoster, it offers a psychological explanation for why he might choose to act this way.

There are certain precautions you can take against ghosting. We want you to feel excited by the prospect of a new man in your life, but we don't want you to get carried away on the first dates. Maintain a levelheaded approach even months after you've officially started dating; it takes years to truly know someone (even when you think you know your partner thoroughly, he can change). Don't plan too far in advance if you aren't completely stable with a person. We've heard clients literally planning their wedding day…after their first date! Follow the flow of the romance and don't raise your expectations if you see that he's not entirely reliable. Protect yourself by remaining optimistic but realistic at all times.

Ghosting stems from doubts and insecurities within, so in all honesty, you probably didn't do anything to make the person stop contacting you. Many times, a ghoster isn't even sure what he wants. He might genuinely like a woman but might not be ready to move in the direction of actual commitment. He might think that contacting her too often will force him into a full-blown relationship. It's also likely that you don't know everything that's going on in his life. So relax and don't overanalyze the situation. Don't blame yourself for circumstances that have little to do with you; you've done nothing to "scare" anyone away. A man who doesn't want you also doesn't deserve you. If it's meant to be, he will come back to you.

Guilt is mentally oppressive. Psychology teaches us that we try to avoid doing things that invoke feelings of guilt. Have you ever lied about falling asleep so you wouldn't have to answer your friend's call and confess that you don't actually feel like going out? Everyone has. Simply avoiding someone is far easier on the mind than trying to explain the reasons why you'd rather not be in touch anymore. A man might prefer to take this route if he no longer wishes to date a woman rather than be blunt and risk hurting her feelings, which would make him feel liable. Is it wrong to do? Yes. Is it human nature to take the easy way out? Yes.

Perhaps what's most frustrating about ghosting is the decision you'll have to make: should you contact him or simply let him go? Ultimately, reaching out to a ghoster boils down to what you intuitively feel you should do. Sit back, take a deep breath, and introspect: do you really like this man or do you just like the idea of being with someone? Are you afraid to call him first because you might be rejected or because your ego's holding you back? It's okay for a woman to make the first move! But it's only worth it if you feel a truly special connection. If you really like someone who's gone missing, don't give up so easily. If you're more afraid of being alone in general, then good riddance.

Ghosting can be baffling and hurt as much as an actual breakup. But if you look at it through a different lens, you can avoid the emotional sting and figure out the right actions to take going forward.

THE SOCIOPATH

The sociopath is not an archetype, but we felt the need to include how to recognize him so that you can stay far, far away. As you know, we believe nearly every man is capable of commitment. But that doesn't mean commitment will come easily to every man; there are men who will have to overcome serious emotional blockages before they're able to give devotion to their partner. The most extreme of these manifests as antisocial personality disorder or sociopathy.

This disorder is more common than we could have imagined. We've met and counseled thousands of patients who had the misfortune of falling in love with a sociopath. That doesn't mean your significant other is a sociopath just because he has issues with commitment. But if you find yourself suffering endlessly because of a man who can't act in good faith, you must be able to recognize the signs.

By definition, sociopathy is a personality disorder that leads to utter disregard for others. A sociopath comes across as likeable and irresistibly charming. Beneath this façade, he uses Machiavellian tactics to get what he wants. A sociopath's first and foremost love is power. His desire is to control, and he's a master of manipulation. A sociopath has no problem lying to, cheating on, or stealing from his partner; psychologically, he feels no remorse for his actions.

A sociopath is a dangerous, callous man. He is a womanizer who will suck his partner dry of her strength and destabilize her mentally and emotionally. Men and women alike can be sociopaths, and any of the archetypes can take on sociopathic traits. Sociopaths are two-faced: the side they show to the world that looks like the epitome of a perfect man and the side they show to the poor individuals who have crossed into their personal space. You can expect the sociopath to act outrageously indignant the moment you accuse him of being anything close to what he really is.

A sociopath will call *you* a sociopath, and he's so persuasive that he'll make you believe it. He'll have you convinced there's something wrong with you, never with him. Simply put, the sociopath wants you to be whatever he wants, whenever he wants. Sociopaths cannot develop emotional bonds that are legitimate and therefore can't engage in normal, functional, or lasting relationships with a partner.

The sociopath's lack of feelings for others allows him to treat people as objects. It's not that he thinks everything revolves around him, but quite simply that nothing is off limits. Because his human conscience is underdeveloped, the sociopath feels no moral compunction to play fair or treat others the way he wants to be treated. So what to you or me seems wrong seems perfectly fine to the sociopath, so long as it helps him get his way.

When you first meet him, the sociopath will have his best face on. This will make you fall head over heels for him. He will have a powerful hold over you, but it won't be a gentle or caring hold; it'll be a domineering, exploitive, and abusive grip. You're more susceptible to the control of a sociopath if you're an authentically kind and giving individual. The sociopath can wreak havoc on any of the seven archetypes. Even the Well-Rounded One will be left reeling after an encounter with a sociopath.

No woman wants to admit that the man she adores is a sociopath, but being honest with yourself will save you. Jennifer was a normal woman who was swept off her feet by a man named Danny. He took her out to the most expensive restaurants in town and called her his "sugar bear," a term of endearment he said he made up just for Jennifer. There was only one tiny problem: Danny was married. He stated that he was in the process of filing for divorce and didn't live in the same house as his soon-to-be ex-wife. He claimed he wanted to be with no one in the world but Jennifer. But Danny's words and actions didn't match up: he only saw Jennifer once a week. He couldn't sleep over Jennifer's house or stay with her for too long, always insisting he had to go do something for his kids. Danny would go missing precisely on every major holiday. If Jennifer got upset, Danny would turn everything on her and make her feel guilty. Jennifer wondered why, if he wasn't committed to his wife, couldn't Danny commit to her?

Jennifer let it slip to Danny that she had saved up some money, and Danny started suggesting that she invest it into his business. Jennifer continued to mute her intuition and go against her better judgment, thinking she could improve her relationship with Danny since he was definitely getting divorced. She was even ready to make a check out to his company, hoping this would make him come closer to her. Her stubborn persistence continued until one day the truth hit her like a brick…being thrown through her window.

Startled, Jennifer jumped up and peered through her shattered window. Danny's wife was standing outside with another brick in her hand. "Come out, Jennifer! We have to talk about Danny!" Normally, Jennifer would have called the police on anyone who damaged part of her property, but right now she felt that could wait; it was more important, finally, to hear the truth.

Jennifer stood outside with Danny's wife for a long time. It turned out that Danny had no intention whatsoever of divorcing. At first, Jennifer didn't want to believe the words coming out of her mouth: that Danny still lived at home with her and their two kids, that they were still having intercourse regularly, and that—apart from Jennifer intruding in their marriage—they shared a lovely relationship. Jennifer wouldn't have believed what this woman was telling her were it not for the fact that she showed Jennifer copious photos and messages that validated her claims. Danny's wife even called Danny in front of Jennifer, and when he picked up he said to his wife, "Hey, sugar bear, where are you? I've been waiting for you at home." After that enlightening conversation, Jennifer deleted Danny's number from her phone, fixed her window, and moved on from her experience with a sociopath.

The sociopath is beyond your help; you cannot do anything for him that will not end up hurting you. If your love interest displays the telltale signs of a sociopath, then please, put down this book, block his number, and pick it up again once you're ready to find a new, more normal partner. Cutting off all contact with the sociopath is the only way to reset your power. We encourage you to walk away now, with your sanity and happiness still intact.

"But how will I know I'm dating a sociopath?" you might ask. Your emotions will betray the truth, as they always do, but you must allow them to reveal it without making excuses for him. Cognitive dissonance is the state of having thoughts or beliefs that are inconsistent with your decisions or actions—when knowing and doing are opposite. Our mind creates dissonance when the truth is too unpleasant to face. You might know cigarettes cause cancer, but that doesn't stop you from lighting one. Likewise, you might instinctively know your partner shouldn't be treating you a certain way, but you don't do anything about it and you stay with him. Applying cognitive dissonance to your relationship with a sociopath may help you "lie" to yourself, but it won't change what you feel: you'll still feel something is horribly wrong. If your partner frequently makes you feel anxious, belittled, hopeless, or depressed, know that he's most likely affected by a sociopathy disorder. Pay attention to the emotions your partner invokes in you and know that your feelings are never wrong; they are superior sources of truth.

You don't want to make a sociopath commit; it will be a long and arduous journey that will cause you undue pain. Unless his personality disorder is treated, the sociopath can give you no genuine form of commitment. He may offer a faint trace of loyalty so that you continue to remain attached, but his attachment will quickly prove to be an illusion. The sociopath must remain in control because the moment he feels the slightest slip in his power, he'll end the relationship.

All people are capable of change, but they have to want to change and undertake the necessary efforts. Sadly, there are no commitment solutions for the sociopathic man who sees no reason to seek help for his disorder. Attracting a partner with such personality problems may be the result of unresolved karma.

Chapter 3

KARMA AND COMMITMENT

*With awareness and the right actions,
you can break out of patterns that have
defined your life long before birth.*
—Carmen Harra

A FAMILIAR SCENE

Your dog sits at the foot of your bed, watching you with benign curiosity as you blow your nose for the umpteenth time. Soggy tissues are scattered across the sheets as you reach for another. Your eyes are red and swollen, your face blotchy. The pain is too profound.

Disillusionment and distress weigh down the hours. You've seen better days than this. You were so sure he was the one, that this time it would be different. Your dog scoots close and nestles up against you. You pet him half-heartedly while consoling yourself: *I guess spending the rest of my life with my dog won't be so bad.* If only people were as unconditionally loving as our four-legged friends!

One way or another, we've all been in the dog scenario before, ready to permanently renounce love after another failed relationship. We understand that right now it feels like doubt and fear have inundated your love life. You wonder what purpose, if any, is behind these constant roadblocks and whether you'll ever escape the vicious cycle of disappointment. While it would be great to have your furry companion around forever, you don't have to spend the rest of your life with just your dog.

But here's the catch: you'll have to break through the karma that erected those roadblocks in order to regain control of your love life and have the relationship you've always wanted. This chapter shows you how to end a cycle that may have started long before you were born.

MEET YOUR KARMA

Your karma is like the third person in your relationship. It's an invisible but ever-present force, always felt but never seen. In fact, it's a force so powerful that it can dictate your love life entirely, from who you meet, to how long you last, to how the relationship plays out.

Karma might sound scary, but once we define it properly, we see that it's nothing to fear. Karma is necessary to maintain order and balance in our world: it is the reaction to every action. It's a much-misconstrued subject and certainly not as elementary as "what goes around comes around." This is a narrow explanation of an elaborate universal principle that doesn't even begin to skim the surface of karma's true nature. The best way to put it is that karma doesn't always give you what you *want*; we're sure you're a good-hearted person who deserves an equally good-hearted partner. No, karma gives you what you *need*—to understand, expand, and evolve. Karma is the memory of your soul, an imprint on your spiritual DNA that materializes throughout your life in the form of people you meet and things that happen to you. Such soulful enlightenment is admittedly painful.

Your karma is yours like your eye color, voice, and blood type are yours. It is attached to your being and belongs to you, although you can't see it the way you see your physical features when you look in a mirror. But karma makes sure that you feel its presence in your life through the repetition of events, situations, and people. It will knock at your door time and time again until you open and say,

"I get it, enough already!" In terms of love, unsettled karma will cause you to experience similar scenarios over and over again, such as meeting the same types of partners and enduring the same heartache, until you become aware and take appropriate action. If your ex cheated on you but you never healed, a new boyfriend is more likely to do the same. If your current partner borrowed money from you that he never returned, he'll probably ask for more (and also won't give it back). Such are the actions that establish karmic patterns. If you want to clear your love karma, you must welcome it in as you would an old (and very annoying) friend. A clean karmic slate sets your soul free to fulfill your many purposes on Earth, and to give and receive boundless love.

If you feel stuck in your love life, unresolved karma may be to blame. Old karma is relentless and exceptionally effective at impairing the progress of relationships. You already know that you can't have a great relationship before you learn your lessons. You're meant to pass through your karma, your partner through his, and you're meant to resolve the karma you share together.

Karma is largely benevolent because it opens your eyes to things you have to solve; it forces you to pay attention to outstanding problems and recurring issues. Without karma to make us feel uncomfortable, our relationships wouldn't advance past a certain point and would become stationary. Recognizing the presence of karma between you and your love interest will lead you to work through it and improve your relationship.

KARMA AROUND-THE-CLOCK

Karma and time are symbiotic: they can work off of each other. Karma can intensify with time, and time can proliferate karma. Karma doesn't subside just because a certain amount of time has passed. On the contrary, the more experiences you go through, the more karma you create. The longer you put off examining and working on your karma, the more it escalates and makes you attract identical situations that don't work out. This is why it's necessary to settle karma that comes from your past before creating new karma.

Karma is a curious mix of fate and free will, a dance between physical and universal. The way we like to look at it is that free will is flawed because it creates negative karma, but fate is perfect because it gives you opportunities to rectify that karma. Karma follows its own clock; you can't put a time on correcting it. It can happen in days, years, or several lifetimes! It depends partly on how much work you put into it, how much karma you have to resolve, and how karma runs its course.

You have to take into consideration divine timing and honor the rhythms of your life. Being in tune with time will help you relieve heavy karma. You don't want to precipitate matters and cause them to happen prematurely, but you also don't want to procrastinate and lose important opportunities. That way, you act when the time is right and stay still when it's not. When it's time to move forward in a relationship, you take action without hesitation, and when it's time to take a step back, you stay still with ease.

Life comes in cycles, and some are ideal for working on your karma. If you pay attention to the signs, you can understand what messages the universe is trying to convey to you. As we like to say, *timing is everything, and everything in time.* The more you're in accordance with divine time, the more you can use it to your advantage and work with it instead of fighting against it.

I, Carmen, based my second book, *Decoding Your Destiny*, on numerology because our personal numbers perfectly explain our lives. Trust us when we say that it's no coincidence you came into this world when you did: the day, month, and year of your birth constitute your life map. Your sacred cycles are an integral part of karmic resolution because they offer you specific opportunities to rectify old karma and generate new karma. You see, your life spans out in cycles of nine years. This means that every nine years, you enter a new phase of existence. Some years are conducive to change, some require us to take action, and others are meant for quiet reflection. Knowing your partner's numbers will reveal where he is now and where he's meant to go, as well as explain the numerological compatibility between you. We encourage you to do a bit of research on life paths and personal years because divine timing is influencing your every step. With this knowledge, you hold the blueprint of your life in your hands!

SOURCES OF KARMA IN RELATIONSHIPS

We all carry some form of karma, and it's usually a mixture of good and bad. You may be wondering where karma comes from. Your karma hails from past lives, and chances are that you've created a bit of new karma through your earthly experiences too. Karma can be shared or "passed down" to you through generations, which means that you didn't actually do anything to earn it. This type of karma is called ancestral karma. It can be encoded in your genes, just like physical traits. This is why a child might take on the same personality as one of his parents, effectively "becoming" his mother or father, even if that parent isn't physically present in his life. You might jokingly say to your mother, "Thanks for giving me your wide hips!" Well, now you can add, "Thanks for giving me your wide hips and karma with emotionally unavailable men!" (We're joking, of course. If this is the case, chances are that it was unknowingly carried over to her too.) In terms of karma you created during this lifetime, it can originate in childhood experiences (especially painful ones) and traumatic events that left a mark on you.

If you want to change a story's ending, you have to revisit its beginning. Understanding your karma requires that you return to the origin: when, where, how, and why did this pattern start? What exactly keeps repeating? Is it that you keep bringing in partners with the same problematic qualities, that you keep hitting the same wall in your relationships, or that they all end in the same awful way? Identify the issue then its source. Did your parents' relationship suffer similarities, or was it something that happened to you as a child? Recognizing the reality of your karma beckons a bit of introspection, but it is the crux of resolution.

You also have free will, of course, so if you don't like your karma, then you have every right to try and change it. Let's say that, according to your family karma, you might go through a divorce in this lifetime. You want to avoid this, so you choose your partner extra carefully and do your best to work out the problems in your relationship instead of separating. In this way, you can alter the course of your karmic destiny. You can utilize free will to counteract your karma or to encourage it; the decision is entirely yours.

You can amend your contract with the universe, but only to an extent: because many of the things written in your karmic code have to happen, they will find a way of manifesting. This is what your soul signed up for! For the most part, you will have to pass through the situations that were set up for you before you reincarnated. These are your individual lessons you agreed to learn. But identifying your karma can tell you what to expect and help you navigate through all of life's twists and turns.

Once you've identified your unique karma, you will have to alter the actions you take. Karma likes to test us by leading us toward the same situations to see if we respond as we did before. If we do, we repeat the karmic cycle. People say that insanity is doing the same thing over and over again and expecting different results. They're right! If you're upset that you keep attracting cheaters, yet you give every notorious cheater a chance, how do you expect to meet an honorable man? Reverting to familiar behavior will keep you stuck in frustrating patterns. You cannot continue to take the same actions and hope for different outcomes; old habits will keep you tied to negative karma. Only new approaches can reap new results.

But what exactly is it that makes us do the same old things, though we don't want to? One factor is the mechanics of our memory. Memory is generally divided into two categories: explicit and implicit. Explicit memory can be verbally expressed, meaning it's made up of things we can easily recall: faces, names, locations, and events. Implicit memory accounts for things we have learned but can't verbalize—things that run on autopilot, like tying your shoelaces or brushing your teeth. This is why you still remember how to ride your bike even if it's been sitting in your garage for a decade. This category of memory operates beyond conscious awareness and is comprised of skills, habits, behaviors, and even addictions. And it's capable of infinite storage! This means you can actually retrieve memories from your infancy or even past lives, if you access the right compartment of your brain. On some far-reaching layer of your mind, you do remember everything your soul has ever experienced. Here, karma merges with science: it is implicit memory that causes you to behave in ways that are unfavorable to you. This branch of karmic memory makes you take actions that have shown to be erroneous, faulty, and painful for you and others. You keep doing these things because they are embedded in your subconscious and familiar to your brain. To change your karma, you will have to interrupt the pattern of acting on certain implicit memories. Making such behavioral modifications calls for self-awareness.

Alicia and Matthew's relationship was in a karmic whirlwind. They loved each other dearly and felt intensely drawn to one another, but every few weeks, a major argument would erupt that would make Matthew pack his bag and leave the house. He always returned a few days later and the couple made up like nothing happened. But Matthew barely had time to unpack his duffel bag properly before the next fight broke out, and he was bursting over the threshold of the door again. Alicia realized she had to do something and fast, as the series of arguments was depleting the couple of hope and energy. So she sat and ruminated: *What role am I playing in these fights and what can I do to prevent them?* There was only one thing left to do: she would have to change her behavior and see if that helped matters.

That Sunday, the opportunity for an argument presented itself as Matthew overslept, leaving Alicia to do the household chores. When Matthew finally woke up and noticed Alicia's brooding expression, he asked, "What now? You're mad over some laundry?" What Alicia would have liked to respond was, "You never help me! You let me do everything around this damn house!" But instead of rebuking Matthew, she remembered her new strategy and stopped her angry retort before it came out. She simply held out the laundry hamper she had been carrying and said, "I'm not upset. I was hoping that maybe you could help me fold these while I make us breakfast."

Matthew's bad mood instantly died away, and he smiled as he took the hamper and walked off to do what his partner had asked.

Alicia and Matthew's regular disputes decreased as the couple became increasingly aware of their behavior. They began creating new and happier memories for themselves, while Matthew's duffel bag was reserved only for vacation.

Expanding your perception and taking different actions will help to clear your karma now, but you still have to discover how it started: with your ancestors, in your childhood, or out of trauma.

ANCESTRAL KARMA

One of Alexandra's favorite poems is "Devil's Daughter" written by Segovia Amil. In it, Amil writes, "There are days my pain is so elaborate...that the salt of my tears tastes not of my own but like that of my ancestors—and the women who dealt with this sorrow before me."

Why are you stuck in the same kind of relationship as your mother was, or her mother before her? Ancestral karma is inherited from people who lived and loved before you and is not your fault in any way. The truth is that feeling scorned, rejected, or betrayed is nothing new. Relationships didn't suddenly begin to involve conflict and suffering during this generation, or the ones before it. Pain seems to have gone hand in hand with commitment since the dawn of time.

You may or may not believe in God or the Bible, but the story of Adam and Eve teaches us a big lesson about commitment: Earth's first inhabitants were ordered to be committed to one other, but they broke their vows almost immediately. Plenty of other ancient tales paint the same picture: classical Greek plays revolve around husband and wife crossing each other then swearing revenge on one other, like Agamemnon and Clytemnestra. Helen, a beautiful woman caught between two relationships, caused the entire Trojan War. And Cleopatra preferred to take her own life rather than live without her beloved Mark Antony. We can go on and on from ancient to modern history, but we think you'll agree that calling relationships "complicated" is an understatement.

The more accurate way to describe them would be *karmic*. The karma that exists in relationships today was created hundreds, if not thousands, of years ago. And the problems you're experiencing in your relationship right now are just bits of global memory playing out again, like the same movie set in a different time or place. But just how far back does the karma go and how is it affecting your relationships? What we've seen is that karma is often passed down from parent to child through generations, until it is recognized and resolved.

Christina called us one evening and said that she wanted to get out of a relationship but didn't know how. She confessed that no matter what she did, she couldn't leave her boyfriend; it was almost as if an otherworldly string was binding them together. Christina wasn't particularly happy with her partner but felt like she had met him for a reason. There was an intense pull from the beginning and the spiritual inkling of having to work through something. She also noted that she found herself in a situation identical to her mother's. When she was younger, Christina's mother had fallen for a very complicated man. He was married with two children. This man was five years older than her, pretty short, decently stocky, and worked as a newscaster for a local station. He also had a wandering eye and a penchant for younger women. Christina's father negated her as his child, and she grew up without him. She stated that this had hurt her a great deal...but then something weird happened. One night, Christina met a man at a social event. He was five years older than her, pretty short, decently stocky, and worked as a newscaster for a local station. He also had two kids and claimed he was in an unhappy marriage. At first, Christina didn't think anything of these "coincidences" and started dating him. But she soon discovered that he had a wandering eye and a penchant for younger women. Christina started thinking at length about the similarities between her boyfriend and her father. What were the odds that Christina attracted a partner so similar, down to the career? And the better question was, why? We explained that it was highly likely that Christina's mother had unfinished karma with Christina's father. This karma got passed down to Christina, and now she had to make a choice: have a child with this man and perpetuate her mother's karma for another generation or muster every ounce of her will and break the cycle by leaving him. We're not sure what decision Christina made, but what we do know is that this is a classic example of ancestral karma.

If you believe a negative commitment pattern (like divorce or abandonment) runs in your family, do a bit of detective work to find out how it first started. Speak to your parents and grandparents about their relationships and find out if they ever passed through some of the problems you're facing in love. Discover how, when, where, and why the imprint started. You'll be surprised at the details you'll unearth and the personal experiences your family members will share with you. Approach this exercise from a place of love: don't judge your family members for any decisions they may have made in their relationships. Understand that at the time, they may not have known better or may not have had another choice. What matters is that you get to the bottom of the karma to reconcile it once and for all.

CHILDHOOD KARMA

Another way that karmic commitment problems arise is out of childhood experiences. They begin at home as we grow up witnessing the dynamic between our parents; their relationship affects our development and conduct. When we see a parent or family member suffering in his or her relationship, we start to view commitment as something negative. Children are highly impressionable, so seeing Mommy crying because of something Daddy did can leave a permanent imprint on them. Children are so sensitive, in fact, that statistics about kids growing up in broken homes are shocking: according to the *Journal of Child Psychology and Psychiatry*, teenagers in single-parent families and blended families are three times more likely to need psychological help within a given year. After they grow up, those who came from broken homes are almost twice as likely to attempt suicide than those who came from homes with both parents, says the *Journal of the American Academy of Child and Adult Psychiatry*. Furthermore, seventy percent of long-term prison inmates grew up in broken homes. This is not to say that children who come from dysfunctional families have to grow up to be dysfunctional themselves. But what we've noticed in our practice is this: children usually end up doing the exact same or the exact opposite as their parents.

The question then becomes, *why would we keep doing what our parents did if it was self-destructive or hurtful to others?* Maybe it's because that's all we know. As we explained, we are creatures of habit who implement memory into action. Because of this, we'll keep repeating what we've learned until we learn otherwise. So even if it's wrong, we will do what we saw others doing. Perhaps we also like to believe that we can make the situation more positive for us than it was for our parents and transform the outcome. Subconsciously, we want to rectify what brought pain to us and those we love. And certainly we can, if we undertake the process of correcting our karma.

As you venture into elementary relationships, you start to experience commitment problems firsthand, like that boy who broke your heart in middle school. You probably look back on such instances of puppy love and laugh, but remember how much your first "relationship" affected you when you were in it! You may have run home crying your eyes out when you saw your crush kissing somebody else on the playground, or you may have been wrought with feelings of inferiority when the boy you liked didn't requite your feelings. These memories are still in you, stored within the explicit and implicit libraries in your brain. Everything you have ever experienced remains with you, a part of you, etched into your being. Everything that happened to you, no matter how insignificant it seems now, had a hand in molding the way you think and act today.

Have you ever noticed that social media apps offer suggestions based on your views and likes? If you were browsing through a page about makeup on Instagram, you might find that the next time you open the app your entire Explore page is filled with makeup artists and the ads selected for you are all for beauty products. This might be a clever algorithm, but it's also a timeless karmic principle that applies to real life: what you experience establishes what you attract.

Out of experiences, sequences of behavior are formed. As soon as you experience something that has a strong impact on you—whether negative or positive—it gets stored in your human hard drive and opens universal doors for similar experiences to follow. This isn't a problem when your hard drive is filled with joyful experiences and happy relationships, because you will bring in more of those. The problem is when it gets jammed with challenges and obstacles that all resemble each other in nature. It is then that patterns become hard to terminate. The only way to shatter a painful cycle is to return to the origin, to the earliest memories stored in your human hard drive.

Think about what you recall from your youth. More often than not, you'll only be able to recall memories that had an impression on you. Do you see your parents playing with you, beaming down at you, or do you hear their arguments and shouts? How did you first learn about commitment? Was it from watching your parents or through a television show? When was the first time that you devoted yourself to something, and what was it (a project, a pet, an idea, a younger sibling, etc.)? Go back to that moment.

Then, evaluate how your idea of commitment has evolved with time and personal experience. What has bolstered your belief in commitment? What has weakened it? How have your views of commitment changed based on your past relationships? Your age or situation in life? Take as much time as you need to answer these questions.

Next, reflect on how you were treated growing up, on whether your opinions were valued or not; how did the people around you make you feel? Did your parents listen to what you had to say when you were little or did they dismiss your feelings? Did your family members, teachers, classmates, and friends advocate your thoughts and beliefs or invalidate them? This has a lot to do with how your sense of self developed: invalidation leads to unworthiness while validation leads to strength. Children who are empowered are more likely to have a strong sense of worth and high level of self-confidence as adults. This plays out positively in their love relationships, as they reject the wrong partners, stand up for themselves, and earn respect more easily.

Acknowledging what emotions you associate with the people in your life can help you figure out the karma you share with them. Think about each of your parents: do you think lovingly of your father? Do you harbor any resentful feelings toward him because he left your mother or wasn't in your life that much? Are you at peace with your mother, or do you blame her at all for being too controlling over your life or putting pressure on you? These are only a few examples of common emotions that people associate with their parents. Unfortunately, such emotions are often the provenance of lifelong karmic patterns.

Your situation could be completely different, and you may have perfect relationships with your parents. But maybe you got stuck in a commitment pattern early on after a partner hurt or left you. Perhaps your crush in high school made you believe that you shouldn't trust men because they're "all the same." Evaluate how you regard your first relationships.

Now think about how the people in your life make you feel in the present moment. If you were often discouraged as a child, do you find that you're still surrounded by people who discourage you today? If you were bullied in school, did you bring in partners who pushed you around as an adult? If one of your parents abandoned you at a young age, do you feel like all of your love interests end up walking out on you? Besides creating karma that will play out in later years, childhood experiences can produce trauma.

TRAUMATIC KARMA

A third source of karma in relationships is trauma: experiences that left you afraid of new relationships, closed off to other people, or doubtful of your future. The definition of trauma is a "deeply distressing or disturbing experience." When we think of trauma, we think of a major life event such as death or serious injury. But even little things can become unsettling, especially if they happen more than once: being let down, being lied to, getting yelled at, getting cheated on, and so on. Even if the trauma isn't considered serious by others, it is serious because it mattered to you. Even if everyone is telling you to "get over it," it still hurt you. It would be more appropriate to start thinking of trauma as something that each of us has endured to some extent.

As you'll learn in the next chapter, pain is your most profound emotion. It strikes more deeply than other feelings and also lingers for a longer time. You might forget about a time when you were happy, but you'll definitely remember a moment that brought you pain. Suffering trauma in relationships is almost guaranteed to create negative karma and commitment problems.

We're incredibly resilient, but we need to heal at every step of life. Healing isn't something we do once then never do again; it's an everyday endeavor. We go through life healing old wounds but not realizing that at the same time new ones are being inflicted. We need to restore harmony within ourselves, specifically after an unhealthy relationship or a difficult separation. Otherwise, our emotions can become permanently distorted and our relationships adversely affected. When we don't heal from our traumas, we spend the rest of our lives either manifesting or rejecting them.

As we worked with our clients throughout the years, we came to understand the most common traumas that form commitment patterns. We're sure you've found yourself in the middle of one, a few, or all of these painful situations:

- Arguing then (you) assuming blame.
- Emotional outbursts then periods of calm.
- Disappearing then reappearing like nothing happened.
- Emotional intimacy then sudden withdrawal.
- Chronic betrayal but staying together.

Any of the seven archetypes can exhibit such trauma-inducing patterns. Trauma is responsible not only for creating chaos in our relationships but for keeping us in those relationships. What keeps us tied to our partner are strong emotions, but strong emotions don't always equal healthy emotions. This means that hate can keep you in a relationship just as much as love can; resentment can make you stay with a person just as much as forgiveness can. Like a never-ending merry-go-round, we replicate the emotions over and over again until we become so used to them that we almost can't imagine having a relationship in which they're not present. It's a terrible thing to hate and love your partner at the same time, but we become used to the bad just as easily as we become used to the good.

Discovering the roots of your relationship traumas entails much contemplation. It takes time, tenacity, and self-conviction above all. Patterns can't be broken in one day because they weren't established in one day. The way you should think about it is this: life consists of many, many phases. An unhealthy commitment pattern may have started during one phase of your life, particularly one in which you experienced trauma. But you've long outgrown that phase. The pattern remains attached to you, but it no longer serves you (it may never have served you to begin with). You have to detach yourself from it little by little, day by day, and create newer, healthier relationship habits. Simple daily actions can help you break free from dependencies: waking up and choosing to go to the gym instead of spending an hour on social media, not responding to your ex's texts, improving your eating habits, letting go of friends who find themselves in similar patterns (because they're enablers), utilizing self-help methods, and much more.

THE MIND-BODY-SOUL OF ENDING PATTERNS

Recognizing and ending karmic commitment patterns require you to be brutally honest with yourself, the way you are when you advise your best friend. There is no shame in wanting to lighten your karma load and liberate yourself from emotional and psychological restraints.

We believe the best way to end the resurgence of old karma is to take action; this is how you transcend from *thinking about doing* to *doing*. Since your karma is integrated into your entire being, it's not just "something you feel" or something that's "in your head." It's something that becomes part of you. The work for removing karmic commitment imprints, therefore, must be carried out on all levels of being: mental, spiritual, emotional, and physical.

In terms of the mental aspect of erasing karma, you can practice your mind's ability to manifest. If you learn to control it, your mind holds tremendous power. And sometimes, you're just one thought away from getting what you want. Negative mental imprints can literally hold you back from your destiny. If the belief that you're not attractive enough is fixed in your mind, you need to change that today. Visualize a nice guy starting a conversation with you or an attractive stranger smiling at you as you walk down the street. Then, when an attractive stranger really does smile at you as you walk down the street, smile back! You will be amazed at what your brain can reel in, good or bad. Train it to focus on positive, productive thoughts that can replace negative imprints. The trick is to concentrate with all your might, like you've never believed anything more than what you're believing right now.

Because karma is a spiritual principle, it can reside in your soul. The best spiritual exercise for removing negative commitment imprints is to hone your intuition as much as possible. Your intuition holds the highest truth. It is your direct divine channel, like a spiritual hotline for help when you're confused or in doubt. A strong intuition can illuminate the right way forward and protect you from getting hurt. Start by trusting yourself with small matters. Don't overthink or overanalyze; go with your first instinct. Then, congratulate yourself for being right! Sharpen your intuitive skills until you build up enough trust in yourself to make major intuitive decisions, including in your relationships. A strong intuition befits you with a keener perception of life. Remember: if something feels wrong, it is.

Cleanse your emotions of karmic traces too. Emotional imprints are like stubborn stains on the heart. Of all impressions, they prove most challenging to remove. The key here is not to try to *remove* the imprints but to pacify the emotions they cause. We like to call this emotional alchemy: converting one emotion into another. If karmic imprints are causing you to feel irascible, stop your anger in its tracks and transform it into a better emotion like acceptance. We're taught to believe that we have no control of our emotions, but we do because they're not separate from us; they are a part of us. The feelings with which you choose to respond can steer any situation in your favor.

We're also told to allow our feelings to run their full course, but this is not always good for us because we can become fixed into one emotion. If you have trouble changing one emotion into another, keeping this in mind may help you: your emotions control your circumstances. If you learn to control your emotions, you can control your circumstances. React in the same manner, and you will meet the same arguments. If you break down and cry in front of your partner for any little thing, he'll notice that you can't control your emotions and might not take you seriously. But if you learn to master your emotions, stand firm, and form a smart response, you have a far better chance of coming to a resolution. You should not disregard your feelings as sources of weakness. All emotions, felt with purpose, can be great resources of strength.

Physically, you can remove karmic commitment imprints by examining your actions. Are you doing things that help or hinder commitment? Are subconscious fears or traumas leading you to act in ways that are detrimental to your relationship? Are you open to new love, or do you block yourself from meeting new people? The most practical way to correct karma is to learn from and take responsibility for your mistakes. When you admit your wrongdoings, you begin to feel your energy shift. Taking responsibility can be difficult to do because your ego doesn't like to be blamed. Start gradually by revisiting past mistakes and strategizing how you'll do things differently when such a situation arises in the future. This is not to say that you should feel guilt or dwell on the past but simply that you promise to consult your karma the next time you're faced with a similar decision. Your actions should reflect awareness and compassion at all times. We know this is easier said than done, but we have full faith that you'll break out of karmic patterns.

FIX THE KARMA, BREAK THE CYCLE

We once had a client named Maria. Maria was a lovely, hardworking woman who just couldn't let go of one particular man. She knew he was no good for her—he rarely saw her and kept stringing her along—but no matter what Maria did, her heart couldn't break away from this person. One day, a special opportunity presented itself to Maria: her job offered to relocate her to a different state. And she accepted, knowing the move would cause her emotional discomfort but be her saving grace at the same time. Maria settled into her new home nicely and her mentality seemed to shift. She was no longer obsessed with the guy who wasn't good for her but was inspired to go out and meet new people. It was only after Maria underwent a positive intervention that she was able to find a much better partner who gave her the attention she wanted.

Sometimes we need an intervention too. We associate the word *intervention* with being admitted to a rehab center because of alcohol or substance abuse. But an intervention can be any action that interferes with a harmful habit and prohibits its recurrence. And it doesn't have to be as drastic as moving out of state; an intervention can be as simple as taking up a new hobby that distracts you from thinking about a person who's not good for you or a daily ritual to enhance emotional clarity. Positive interventions can remove you from karmic cycles that impede love, happiness, and fulfillment. We suggest that you perform small actions each day that reflect your intention to change.

To carry out a positive intervention, you must come to terms with your current situation. Right now, your relationship may involve much struggle and confusion, but trying to evade it won't help you resolve it. Accept what's happening with a calm mind and courageous heart. "Fighting the tide" will cause you to sink, and avoiding your fate will only make you meet it again down the road. Relinquish your resistance and fear, as these emotions only prolong your karma. You'll be surprised at how powerful you'll prove to be against the things that scare you the most! Your obligation to be present holds true through both good and bad, so stand tall and face each moment.

Increase fearlessness by learning how to ground yourself. Refocus on the present when you get carried away by yesterday's sorrows or tomorrow's worries. Sit or stand with your feet planted firmly into the ground and clear your mind. If possible, stand outside barefoot and allow the energy from the earth to rise through you. Place your hands on something (a table, wall, or tree). Concentrate on how that object feels, on its surface, size, and texture. Run your palms across it. Breathe slowly and notice what you smell in the air: is it plants, food, or a candle? What do you hear: the TV, birds chirping, or kids playing? What do you taste on your tongue? Immerse your five senses to reel yourself back into the present. You are exactly where you need to be.

As you accept your present, you can start to project a better future. No matter what you're going through, you can always choose to adopt a more positive outlook. This helps you feel in control of what's to come instead of feeling anxious about it. Allow yourself to daydream, imagining the best possible outcome for your efforts and the most favorable solution to your problems. Also perform actions that are reflective of the good things you're planning. If you have a date coming up, buy yourself a brand-new outfit that shows off your assets. Your mind is a magnet for the outside world, steadily manifesting your thoughts. Preparing for love increases its likelihood.

Small, symbolic acts performed with mindfulness and meaning can reshape your karmic reality. Close your eyes and inhale deeply, feeling your core fill up with fresh air. Hold your breath for a few seconds then exhale slowly. As you exhale, imagine any dark, pent-up energy being released from your being. Affirm to yourself, "I am letting go of old karma that has held me back from finding true love," and, "I welcome a relationship with endless possibilities into my life." If you're already in a relationship, you can say, "I'm sending bad karma back where it began. I'm free to manifest love, loyalty, and joy in my relationship." This breathing exercise is one of the many rituals you can repeat each day to move out stagnant karma and clear your path toward commitment.

Because you are the co-creator of your life, you can influence the course of events once you've learned to calm your mind and control your thoughts. Do this by remembering what went right, not wrong. You may have gone through a turbulent relationship, but you managed to come out unscathed. You may have met some bad people, but you also met a lot of good ones. Obsessing over negativity creates a disproportion in your thoughts, placing emphasis on heavy, fearful ones. Remind yourself of all the times you were divinely protected and spared from something truly bad. This will break the pattern of fretting over the future.

Once you stop worrying, you're free to welcome in new joys. Allow happiness to return to you in new forms: a new man who excites you or a new chapter in your relationship. Never put conditions on being in good spirits or having continued faith. Even if you're experiencing issues in your love life, you have many other reasons to feel fulfilled. The ability to expand and multiply your happiness is entirely yours because joy is your birthright.

One of the best ways to eradicate negative karma is to create positive karma in its place. The principle behind good karma is to do to others what you want done to you. This is known as the Golden Rule in every major religion, from Christianity to Judaism to Islam to Hinduism. When it comes to love karma, this translates into not interfering in other people's relationships, not getting involved with someone who's already taken, and treating your partner with consideration and respect. Be careful not to succumb to situations that create negative karma, like retaliating against lovers who have caused you pain, acting on your ego to get your way, or leaving a lot of loose ends in a relationship. Always ask yourself, "Am I doing what I would want done to me?" When in doubt, follow the Golden Rule.

As you complete these actions, you'll be ready to generate a positive shift in your love life. Change forces you to remain present and take action. Don't be afraid to make the improvements you've been putting off: move to a new location, go back to school, get a better job, find different friends, finish your project, and so on. There's no better feeling than a shift in scenery! Staying in the same environment will cause you to revert continually to the past. But seeking fresh prospects and hopeful opportunities will teach you to honor each precious moment in time.

Your karma may be part of you, but it's a part you have the liberty to change. Follow these steps to transition out of karmic cycles, clear old love patterns, and uphold a healthier relationship.

WHY CAN'T I LET HIM GO?

Karma makes for some intense relationships. We've seen karmic bonds that were nearly impossible to break! In hearing hundreds of different experiences each year, one sticks out in particular: Courtney had just gone through a bitter divorce. Her ex-husband was loaded with money, so she was awarded a fair share of it. Courtney was a smart, successful, and beautiful woman and she could have any man now that she was free. Or could she? Courtney dated a few guys after her separation and got into a couple of relationships, but none had an effect on her like Brad. Brad was a regular guy and the coach of a local basketball team. But Brad had a hold over Courtney like no other man. Courtney and Brad only dated for several months, but Courtney thought about him endlessly. She couldn't get him out of her head, even after she had started a relationship with a new man. When Courtney called us, it wasn't to talk about her new partner—her woes still revolved about Brad. She wondered whether he missed her, what he was doing, and if he was seeing anyone. One day Courtney heaved a deep sigh and asked, "Why can't I let him go?"

We've seen other cases like this, of course. We've seen partners who still longed for each other years after they separated. We've seen marriages that lasted a lifetime because both partners held onto each other and never let go, despite the magnitude of their problems. But this still doesn't explain *why*; why are we able to walk away from some partners but never others? Why are there people who fill us with such desire that we wouldn't leave them for anyone or anything in the world? Even if they don't treat us the way we should be treated, or they cause us harm, we still can't turn our backs on them.

We're certain you've experienced at least one relationship like this. It's likely that you couldn't quite put your finger on it, but there was something…something that kept you glued to this person. The connection might've felt like magic, because it was something not of this world.

So what is that force that makes a relationship last, indifferent of a person's archetype? Money and status can keep two people together, but we're looking beyond physical aspects. Having children can keep a couple from splitting up, though the partners may want to separate if they're unhappy. No, we're referring to the one unbreakable energy that is, of course, karma. If you share karma with the man you love, your relationship won't be so easy to end. You can be with an archetype that's incompatible to yours, yet an invisible string will keep you together. You can be in love with a complicated partner and want to run away from him at times, but if you share mutual karma, nothing but a near apocalypse will break you up.

Karma impacts your destiny by not only bringing you but keeping you close to certain people. It makes you believe in and fight for one man, though he may be complex, egoistic, stubborn, traumatized, or closed-off. It's like an energetic magnet, so that you find yourself so drawn to a person that your desire for him defies all logic. Karma supersedes physical attraction because it belongs to the memory of your soul. Because karma dwells in the depths of your spirit, it has an almost supernatural hold over the decisions you make in a relationship. If you discover that you're in love with one of the more problematic archetypes, like the Narcissist or the Free Spirit, but you just can't let him go, know that your ties may be karmic. You might be thinking that being soul mates or twin flames is what makes you inseparable, but those couples share karma too. And many couples who aren't soul mates remain together because they're bound by karma. Truly, karma plays an undeniable role in commitment.

This doesn't mean that karma is present in every relationship, but that relationships in which there exists old or past life karma are harder to break than ones in which there is new or no karma. It also doesn't mean that the karma you share with your partner is negative, or that you'll have to overcome difficult feats together. Karmic or not, all relationships seem onerous at times.

Depending on what you're meant to go through, the karma you have with your loved one can be a source of immense fulfillment. It may be to meet again in this life and experience the same beautiful relationship you had in prior lives. It may be to build, create, travel, and have children. Only you can discover the karma you share with your significant other because it's privy to your two souls.

Chapter 4

WHEN LOVE HURTS, LOVE YOURSELF

No one will give you what you can give yourself.
—Alexandra Harra

Why do we get into relationships that hurt? Why do we fall in love with people who cause us harm? Because we can't help whom we love; we just do. No one wants to put up with a man who's narcissistic or wounded, no one wants to have complicated relationships, but sometimes love is beyond our control. When love starts to hurt, it's not always an indication to run away from the person we're with or the relationship we're in. It's simply a sign to take a step back and love ourselves for a little while.

You picked up this book because you're either having issues with your partner or you're looking for a dedicated partner. If you find yourself in the middle of a love crisis, whether you're newly single or in a convoluted relationship, this chapter will start you down the road of self-commitment. We're shifting the focus back on you, helping you first to mend your delicate heart and fulfill your own needs before tackling the test of love again.

Before you can be ready for a committed relationship, you have to do a little work. This is an essential step that many people like to skip over: understanding themselves and performing the inner work that makes a relationship with another person possible. Some of us think that our partner is the one with a problem, or we simply think we've done enough work and there's no need to improve ourselves further. Others of us don't think we have to do any work at all, but those are the kinds of assumptions that in the past didn't allow good relationships to prosper.

Here, we focus on some of the work you have to do by yourself and for yourself. This includes overcoming subconscious fears, understanding psychological complexities, and moderating inbred character flaws that stand between you and the commitment you want to have.

It's interesting to note that countries where people get married at young ages are also countries with the highest divorce and separation rates. Second marriages tend to last longer because both partners are wiser and more prepared. It takes time, edification, and a lot of practice to learn how to be in a successful relationship; you have to pass through your lessons first.

You may not want to learn more lessons, or you may think you've learned your fair share, but in order to have a good relationship, you have to have your power intact. This means developing an impenetrable sense of self. Your true power is awakened only in the face of adversity; it is magnified when you confront your challenges instead of allowing yourself to become consumed by them. We want you to learn how to tap into your power so you can shift your circumstances. Only by struggling through relationships can you learn how to be successful in them. And although there's no set formula for having a healthy relationship, we believe this comes as close to it as anything: *to get the love you deserve, you must take back your power.*

This chapter will help you recognize your inherent power and reinforce it to improve the dynamic of your relationships.

BALANCING THE INNER AND OUTER

There exist two kinds of love in this world: love for yourself and love for another person. The key to joyful relationships is learning to weigh your inner and outer energy with great care; invest too much in your partner and you may surrender your self-worth to another.

Invest too much in yourself and you can easily become self-absorbed and egocentric. It's not an easy balance to maintain, but it's crucial to commitment. Ironically, we find it easier to understand and forgive others than ourselves: when someone we love messes up, we hand out forgiveness like a free pass. But when we mess up, we take a long time to forgive ourselves. Why is that?

We put up with what we shouldn't when we're deficient in self-love. Our self-love should be unconditional—as should all love—but not egoistical so that it shuts out regard for others. You must find the happy medium between taking care of your needs as well as your partner's needs. Relationships involve a certain amount of power that has to be divided evenly for them to be healthy.

One large part of maintaining this balance is learning how to delegate your emotions: when to guard them and when to allow access to them. Vulnerability is a beautiful thing, but not so much that it leaves you exposed to negativity. Keep your emotions locked when you sense danger, for they are the gateway into you. Know when to engage and when to refrain from engaging your emotions. If you engage your emotions in minor situations, like for any little argument, you risk harming both your feelings and your relationship. When you feel provoked, take a moment to self-inquire: *What reaction would benefit me most right now? Is it to respond with anger or ignore the situation?* Sometimes the best response is no response, especially until everyone has calmed down.

You must also know when to stop offering help to a person. Just because you love your partner doesn't mean you can fix all his problems for him or piece together his life, especially not at the expense of your own well-being. Your stability should remain intact no matter what your partner is going through. Even if you fit into one of the more sacrificial archetypes, knowing when to say "no" is crucial, not just for your sake but for your partner's; if you always run to his rescue, he won't learn how to resolve his own issues. Learn when you should offer a helping hand and when you should stand back and let him handle it. If it jeopardizes your mental, emotional, physical, or financial soundness, don't do it. Set limits for your sacrifices and stick to them.

A SOLID SENSE OF SELF

Of the two kinds of love that exist, only one is permanent. As Oscar Wilde wrote, "To love oneself is the beginning of a lifelong romance." Love relationships and friendships fade away, and you can even sever ties with a sibling or parent, but your relationship with yourself lasts for the duration of your life. There is no escaping yourself. And the quality of that relationship determines the quality of all other relationships.

If you want to have joyful relationships with other people, you must have a healthy relationship with yourself, what we call a healthy sense of self. This doesn't mean selfishness. It means respecting yourself and allowing yourself to get close to others while also keeping your own identity intact.

Another reason why you need to build a sturdy foundation for yourself is so you don't *become* the person you're dating. It's easy to turn into your partner, emulating both his strengths and weaknesses. If your partner lies, you may learn how to lie from him. If your partner is highly motivated in his work, you may be spurred to work harder in your own career. He may influence you to do things you don't notice but that are obvious to your family and friends.

We don't realize just how much of our partner's personality seeps into ours. A significant other can even change our taste buds! According to a study published in the journal *Appetite*, partners become more congruent over time in terms of taste and smell preferences. It's normal to a certain degree to mold ourselves after someone we care about and see so often, but we shouldn't let our love for the person alter our character. We shouldn't forego our integrity or jeopardize our inner force. If you've developed your sense of self and secured it as thoroughly as possible, you run less risk of losing your essence to your partner.

Everyone goes on and on about self-love, but everyone forgets that it's useless to love yourself if you don't *like* yourself first. Love and like are markedly different concepts. You may love your partner, family members, and friends, but you may not necessarily *like them*; maybe they annoy you or you don't particularly care for their character.

The same principle applies to you. Of course you love yourself; if you didn't, you wouldn't have picked up this book to increase joy in your relationships. Too often we put more effort into developing a relationship with another than into fortifying a relationship with ourselves. We rarely check in on how we're feeling. Do you like who you are? Are you okay with your million peccadillos? Do you accept yourself unconditionally? Do you forgive yourself for faults and flaws that you would surely forgive in others?

To put it another way, have you healed your inner conflicts? These are questions you must ask and answer each day as you journey through various experiences. They'll provide a roadmap in self-acceptance and forming a solid relationship with yourself so you can have it with another person.

Before anyone else can commit to you, you must commit to yourself. This means showing yourself the dedication you want your better half to show you and becoming the kind of person you want to be in a relationship with. Through this, your authentic self will start to shine. You must treasure this special alliance with your higher self; it is a relationship more sacred than any other. Then, you can enter a relationship with self-acceptance and a healed heart—rewards that come when you're thoroughly dedicated to yourself.

LEARN TO BE ALONE

Once you enjoy your own company, no one else's can compare. What's that statement doing in a book about commitment to another person?

Most people dread the idea of being alone, but without that ability, it's very hard to be in a close relationship with another. Too many of us want to have a relationship because we fear solitude. Solitude, however, is key to healing ourselves. Our ability to be alone and to rely on ourselves helps disestablish the false notion that happiness is impossible without a relationship. Self-support sets up the groundwork for a great relationship: you'll be loving without being controlling, attached without being needy, and tolerant without being naïve. If you can be content on your own, a great relationship will add to your joy, but it won't be your only source of joy. You won't need that other person to fulfill all your needs. Instead, that person will complement your existing happiness and vice versa. This is what a truly balanced relationship looks like. If we don't do the positive work on the inside, the strain will show in our other relationships.

Your power to feel joy—with or without a partner—is always within you, but that power has been smothered under the heavy weight of "if" and "when:" I'll be happy *if* or I'll be happy *when*. We're always waiting to be happy. We're always setting conditions for our happiness. Happiness is always arriving around the corner tomorrow, but tomorrow never comes.

The more your life is determined by external influences, the less control you have over it; you experience a frustrating discord between fantasy and reality. In your constant search for happiness, you may have forgotten that you hold the greatest power: the power to remove the "if" and the "when" and simply say, "I am happy."

Allow your joy to surface. Rely on your natural strengths and wisdom. Don't model yourself on what others think, say, or do. If you remember nothing else from this book, at least remember this: *no one will give you what you can give yourself.* If you truly believe and understand that, then your foundation for a relationship is rock solid.

What's the point of commitment if it brings you suffering? As we like to say, "If it brings more pain than joy, be wise and set it aside." Most people, at one time or another, find themselves in a situation like this. If you've been through a slew of bad relationships and feel exhausted, choose not to be in a relationship for a while or choose to take a break from the relationship you're in. Return to yourself, start from there, and see what you discover.

Too many of us are so desperate to have *someone* in our lives that we put up with relationships that are heavily one-sided. If your commitment to a person is causing you mental, emotional, spiritual, or (in many cases) physical anguish, it's time to leave and start a relationship with yourself.

VICTIM TO VICTOR

To heal from your past and finally find commitment, you must stop believing that you're a victim. You were never a victim, no matter how badly you were mistreated or what was done to you. That you find commitment to be hard doesn't make you a victim; it makes you realistic about relationships. Stop thinking that there's something wrong with you; stop telling yourself that you're broken or damaged. Believing otherwise will keep you trapped in self-pity and a low state of energy. Establish this with yourself right now: *I am not a victim.* You are a victor because you overcame your obstacles, oppressive as they were. Applying this mindset is the first change you must make to rediscover the miracle that is love.

We can promise you that you will get what you want, but maybe not when you want it. Sooner or later, something absolutely divine will happen for you: the relationship you deserve, the commitment you've always wanted, or the man you've been dreaming of. But these things can only materialize once you're healed and whole. The sooner you change the inside, the sooner the outside can change.

Your biggest problem is not that love is a challenge. Love is complex, riddled with confusions and seemingly unsolvable predicaments. None of us can get around that. It's impossible to find joy in love at all times, and even the best relationships will be challenged.

No, your biggest problem is that you're looking on the *outside* for the solution, when it has been *inside* you all along. Yes, the love you need is already within. Another person can't and won't supply it for you. You can only share your love with someone else. The love you long for someone else to show you is a love you will have to show yourself. Another person can only mirror what's already in you. Our virtues are meant to be complemented by a partner, not created by a partner. Right now, you hold the full potential to attract the right partner or repair your current relationship. But you must perform your inner work: separate the past from your present, gain a solid sense of self, and learn to be happy on your own.

We all have some healing to do. Even if you've had a relatively happy life, there are still certain elements of you that must be mended. A healed heart makes a night-and-day difference. You experience the world differently when you're whole. When you're broken, you attract broken people and hardship in your relationships. If you're hurt, sick, or stuck, you're not the most complete version of you. You can't give someone else the best of you, and you also can't receive the best of someone else. But when you're whole, life and love flow much more smoothly. You act from the seat of compassion and understanding, so you make wiser decisions that lead to better outcomes for you and others. You vibrate at your highest frequency, achieving your goals with ease and grace. You treat people and the world with greater respect and reverence, and all these positive actions are returned to you tenfold. *Only when you're well on the inside can you welcome in blessings.*

So you see, healing and having a great relationship go hand in hand. We all have subconscious fears, psychological complexities, and inbred character flaws, although we tend to think we're the only ones who have them. You must commit to understanding and healing these fears, complexities, and flaws. The wisdom of healthy relationships is that if you do the work on the inside, you'll find a partner on the outside who can magnify your strengths and mitigate your weaknesses.

You've probably already learned this truth although you may not want to admit it. If you can't feel joy on your own, you won't find joy in another person. If you feel there's no hope in you—if it's been lost, taken away, or not yet discovered—you'll attract a miserable person and a lifeless relationship. If you're constantly reliving the wounds of your past, you'll develop a sense of unworthiness.

The antithesis to self-love is unworthiness—that nagging sense of impotence or diminished purpose. We know what it's like not to be able to change a person or situation; it's one of the worst feelings! We fall victim to our circumstances, feeling regret, guilt, and plunging self-worth. We think, *If only I had done things differently*, or, *I should have known better.* When a relationship fails, we quickly enter a mode of self-criticism. We get sucked into a spiral of shame that makes us feel inadequate and incapable.

Angela always felt inferior to the women in her social circle who were diving into romances with wealthy, high-profile men. She tried to follow in their footsteps and go after the same type of guys but ended up having to put up with a lot nonsense from the wrong kinds of partners. She was powerless in her relationships; the men she dated liked her for qualities she only pretended to have. Angela's life changed when she finally woke up and said, "I give up! I'm going to be myself, and I don't care if they like it or not." As you can guess, Angela found a stable relationship as soon as she faced the reality of her strengths and weaknesses, allowing her unique traits to shine forth.

Holding onto the wrong thoughts, habits, and assumptions, we enter into a cycle of self-blame that becomes increasingly difficult to end. Worse, this feeling of unworthiness can seep into our relationships and strain bonds. We may start blaming our partner for our shortcomings, taking things out on him, or misinterpreting what he's saying and doing. This is why you must enter a relationship with a steady sense of self-acceptance and a healed heart, both of which are birthed from knowing yourself.

MORE POWERFUL THAN PAIN

The German philosopher Friedrich Nietzsche said that "to live is to suffer, to survive is to find meaning in the suffering." We would like to add that not only to survive but to heal is to find true meaning in our suffering. The reality is that many of us don't heal; we make it through our hardships, yes, but we let the pain linger. In our efforts to get over the pain, we bury it into our subconscious mind, but we don't take the time to nurse our wounds. We don't put ourselves together again before proceeding into our next relationship. We must not only move forward but make sure that we're moving forward fully healed. It is in this way that we become more powerful than pain.

Gaining power over your pain means gaining control over your emotions. It means building the strength to walk away from a dangerous partner or overcoming an ordeal that caused exceptional agony. To process emotions in a healthy way, allow yourself to feel your pain, frustration, anger, sadness, or whatever else you're feeling. Instead of stifling the emotion, let it flow through you. If you're feeling overwhelmed, take several slow, deep breaths. Deep breathing helps regenerate tissue, increases the circulation of lymphatic fluid, and promotes better function of the respiratory system. With each slow inhalation, you'll feel your entire body fill up with new and pure energy. As you exhale, imagine the emotional toxicity being pushed out by your breath.

There are many emotion-management tools you can try, from scribbling down your feelings to physical activities like vigorous exercise. When you're angry, we welcome you to beat the life out of a pillow (a pillow, not a person).

Affirmations for mood control are also effective. Whenever you feel yourself getting carried away by a certain negative emotion, repeat to yourself, "I choose to surrender my [choose a negative emotion] and replace it with [choose a positive emotion]. I banish [negative emotion] from my heart, mind, and soul. I choose to nurture love, abundance, health, and faith within me."

LEARNING TO LET GO OF YOUR PAST

*Forgiveness gives you back the power
that was taken from you.*
—Alexandra Harra

To forgive is to live and live well. Know that no matter what happened, you always have the ability to make yourself whole again, and it starts by forgiving. Choose to infuse each day with forgiveness. By practicing forgiveness and detachment, you unburden, unblock, and unbind your life and, by extension, your relationships. Please don't take it personally if someone's harmed you in some way. Bear in mind that people are dealing with issues you know nothing about. This simple logic puts their actions in a different perspective. By disengaging you from harmful thoughts and behaviors, forgiveness shifts the course of your life. It sets you free from suffering and liberates you to seek new opportunities.

No one can hurt you if you forgive them because forgiveness takes away their power and returns it to you. When you forgive, you regain control of your decisions. Forgiveness breaks down hardened karma and detaches the past from you. It helps you move forward by gifting you with wisdom, resilience, and new drive.

One ubiquitous character flaw that all people need to work on is their inability to forgive. It's easy to recommend, not so easy to do. But you can't hope to foster an enriching relationship until you've forgiven everyone, including yourself. Commitment can only come once you've relinquished all resentment.

Resentment doesn't just cripple healthy relationships; it can also harm you physically. Emotions are more than fleeting feelings; they're the building blocks of health. Learning to accept, process, and ultimately master your emotions will restore your mind-body-spirit harmony. Letting go of all things that don't bring you joy—people, thoughts, and situations—may be hard to do, but it can be lifesaving.

Staying in a place that carries heavy emotions stands in the way of a positive future. Sometimes the best way to forgive and detach is to remove yourself from an environment that's burdened by karma from the past. One of our clients was so devastated by her husband's betrayal that she developed cancer as a consequence of her suffering. After she divorced, our client continued living in the same house and suffering from the same illness. The energy of a particular experience can attach itself to a place and trap us both physically and emotionally in the pain of the past. We advised her to move, let go of this ordeal, and start over. As our client settled into her new home, her health not only started to improve, but she even met her other half! Don't be afraid to leave behind a place that's energetically depriving you of health and happiness.

Another one of our clients, Susan, is a lovely ninety-four-year-old lady who's well and thriving. She revealed to us that her secret to a long life has been letting her problems go. Susan doesn't obsess over dilemmas but simply prays for them to be resolved and moves on with her life. "I never held things inside," she said. "I never let the little things bother me, or even the big things at that. I was always peaceful and accepting no matter what was going on, and I showed my problems the way out the door!" Susan shows us that we can live in the moment at any age.

Being present is a decision you get to make. They say that time heals all wounds, but this isn't always true. We're under the impression that time erases our pain and smooths over the damage done to us, when in reality time can carve our emotional scars more deeply. You might be thinking, *Well, I got over that relationship a long time ago!* or, *That bad experience was years ago, so I'm definitely healed from it.* You may or may not be, and you won't know until you introspect without fear of what you might find. You must let things go in order for them to come to an end. *You* have to do it, not time—time won't do anything for you except push the memories down into your subconscious, where they still exist. If you continue to hold on to something, even if it happened a decade ago, it's still very much alive for you. It's still present in your mind and heart and will continue to be present in your reality.

It's easy to advise you to stop your own suffering. We cannot magically pull ourselves out of our misery; if we could, our world would look a lot different! But trust us, you *can* forgive, and it takes less effort than you think. Simply choosing to engage more positive emotions jump-starts the process.

FOUR TRUTHS TO FORGIVENESS

These four truths will help you better understand the virtue of forgiveness and figure out how to forgive in a way that resonates with you. As we go through each of them, reflect on what they mean for you.

Count your blessings first. To forgive what went wrong, you first have to be grateful for what went right. Only when you measure the distance between where you were and where you are now do your blessings become clear. Summarize the lessons you've learned. You are not who you were when you naively trusted someone, or when you gave too freely to a partner who didn't deserve it. Counting your blessings shows you the long way you've come.

Find a reason to forgive. The secret is finding that one reason to forgive. Maybe you want to be strong for your children and set the right example. Maybe you want to prove that you're better than the person who hurt you. Or maybe you simply want to grow as a person and give up old habits. Think about how it would benefit you to forgive. Does a not-so-peaceful past continue to interfere in your present? Do the effects of a former betrayal, breakup, or broken heart continue today? Think about how it would benefit you to forgive by recognizing your personal reasons and motivations. Identify the who, what, when, and why. Then you can begin the process.

Forgiveness takes time. Forgiveness isn't something that comes automatically. It's a philosophy we adopt over time, a process, not a result. You cannot instantly forgive someone—if only it were that easy! You can achieve forgiveness, step-by-step, day by day, through small actions that are in line with your intentions.

Forgive yourself. As with all things in life, forgiveness begins at home. You must be at peace with yourself in order to foster positive relationships. This is done by making peace with your mistakes, however costly they may have been.

ACTIONS TO ERASE REGRET AND RESENTMENT

Who hasn't thought, *If only I had done X instead of Y.* It's all speculation, of course, because we'll never know how things would've turned out if we had chosen X. Looking back, the right decision looks obvious. Yet it wasn't that simple at the time. Many people regret divorcing at first, but later come to realize that it was for their own good. Trial and error are conducive to change: we learn through mistakes. But we must be careful not to dwell too much on our errors or we risk getting stuck in the past, out of tune with time. The truth is that it's all too easy to get stuck in something that happened in the past: a memory, a false belief, a relationship that ended, or an argument that happened long ago. Brooding over the past weakens your potential in the present and blocks new opportunities from reaching you. Holding onto old feelings or habits breeds stagnancy and dissatisfaction.

An anonymous quote reads, "You can't reach what's in front of you until you let go of what's behind you." We couldn't agree more. You can't step forward by looking backward, just like you can't reach for the goal in front of you if your hands are tied behind your back. Living in the present requires self-mastery. But its rewards are invaluable: peace of mind and greater understanding. After all, you exist in this very moment, not one hour ago or in two weeks from now. And you deserve to step into your future without anything holding you back.

Letting go of the past and living in the present is the first act of self-commitment. This encompasses forgiveness and acceptance. To break through your subconscious fears and finally advance in your relationships with others, you must consciously choose to forgive your past, to reflect on it acceptingly rather than regretfully. These are two distinct emotions: when you regret, you resentfully reject a part of your history—a part of you—but when you reflect, you understand where you went wrong, accept what happened, and promise not to repeat mistakes. You forgive others and unload the weight of the past.

Maybe you're afraid of experiencing the dread stirred up by certain memories. It's okay to feel pain; it is just as much a part of life as any other emotion. "The great object of life is sensation—to feel that we exist, even though in pain," wrote the Romantic poet Lord Byron. Pain is an emotion you must fully experience, without looking away. The more you run from it, the more closely pain will follow you. There's no evading it. Unprocessed pain gets buried deep within your subconscious, creating negative karma and resurfacing at the worst times and in the worst ways. Better to let pain run its course naturally.

Don't focus only on the hurt that others have caused you. The less you take personally the actions of others, the less they can affect you. If right now you find yourself hurting, then by all means embrace your pain; be proud of yourself for being courageous enough to feel the most profound emotion available to us as human beings. Cry if you're upset and yell if you're angry, knowing that your suffering will make you stronger. Pain deserves as much attention as joy, perhaps more. Pain can fuel your creativity and ingenuity. It lends you compassion for others and incredible wisdom. The art of living is to allow your pain to come and go without holding onto it, thereby turning it into progress.

You must also put yourself in the other person's shoes, as hard as that may be to do. Forget about your argument, valid as it is, and think about how the other person rationalizes their thoughts, words, and actions. Can you see why he or she acted in a certain way or said certain things?

We're usually not aware of the subconscious trauma or unprocessed emotions that people hide inside. We don't know their full histories, life experiences, or painful memories. But if we bear these things in mind, we can forgive more easily. If you're suffering from a broken heart, seek solace in your natural talents. When you feel pain, create: start a blog about relationships, write a love song, or make a work of art that speaks of resilience. Utilize the insight and sensitivity that come with pain to enrich your life.

TURNING THE WHEELS OF FORGIVENESS

The best way to start the process of forgiveness is to acknowledge who has hurt you and determine how you can heal yourself. Even if someone hurt you when you were very young (whether mentally, emotionally, or physically), the memory can still rear its ugly head in adulthood and affect your relationships. The term dissociative amnesia refers to memories we consciously push down into our subconscious, meaning we "choose" to forget them. It's a phenomenon by which we block out certain events or phases of life, particularly those that caused distress or trauma. So you might not remember the week you spent in the hospital recovering after a bad car accident or the way the kids in elementary school bullied you. Contrary to simple amnesia, the memories from dissociative amnesia still exist, and this poses a problem: they can be revived, often suddenly, under certain circumstances. Your relationship can be moving along nicely, then something in your surroundings can trigger flashbacks of the abuse you suffered in a relationship long ago. This can bring back old feelings of anxiety or insecurity that have no place in your current relationship and drive a wedge between you and your loved one.

This is why it's so important to sort through your warehouse of memories and appease the harmful ones and the people who caused them. Here's an exercise to forgive a person who has hurt you. Starting with your earliest memories, create a list of the people you still need to forgive. Then, pick one from the list. This can be a former friend, lover, or family member—anyone with whom you share unresolved ill will. Write his or her name on a separate piece of paper.

Underneath the name, write the words you associate with this person or how you feel about him or her right now. Don't inhibit yourself, let out everything on paper. Breathe deeply and allow all emotions to rise to the surface, even the ones buried at the bottom. When you're finished, write "I forgive you." If you need to, write this phrase more than once. Fold up the paper and hold it tightly in your hand. Feel as the negative emotions within you are transcribed to this object; they are leaving you. Then, dispose of the paper. You can tear it up and toss it in the trash or burn it. This action symbolizes that you discharge the negative emotions from your being and that you truly let go.

You can repeat this exercise as frequently as it takes to initiate forgiveness. Pay attention to how your emotions are shifting and the words you're choosing as you focus on the memory of this particular person again. Do you feel a little less angry or hurt each time you recall him or her to mind? Do you feel a bit more peaceful with the memory of what happened?

Continue to breathe deeply as your energy elevates. You'll feel lighter as the weight of harmful feelings starts to lift. Say a prayer of forgiveness, asking the divine to help you abandon animosity.

THE THIRTY-DAY MIND-AND-SPIRIT DETOX CHALLENGE

This exercise is a detox for your mind and spirit, and the perfect chance to establish the genuine connection you need to have with yourself before you can share it with another. Chances are that you've already had to go through a similar experience when COVID-19 forced us into quarantine. If so, reflect on how you felt spending increased time alone and being able to do more things for yourself: What has it taught you about your relationship with yourself? Throughout this exercise, we want you to assess what you do out of obligation for others versus what you do that makes you happy. Keeping that in mind, try to do the following activities as often as possible for the next thirty days.

Cook for yourself and make dishes that you—not others—love to eat. If you're not a good cook or you don't like to cook, eat out by yourself. Ask for a table for one, put away your phone, and dine with yourself. Don't rush; chew slowly and savor your food. Thank your body for its amazing ability to taste. Observe the interactions of others. As you pick up bits and pieces of dialogue, muse on the common thread that runs among us: we're all here to love and be loved.

Work out by yourself, or if you attend a public gym, don't pair up with your usual gym buddy. Focus on your power during your workout; feel your many muscles flexing, contracting, and relaxing. Notice how your body responds to your commands. Concentrate on each physical sensation as you move.

Walk outside at least a few times a week by yourself, absorbing the scenery around you. Leave your phone at home or turn it off during this time. Unless the weather is inclement, don't make excuses not to spend time among nature.

Drive by yourself without listening to your usual radio stations or playlists. Instead, find random stations and listen to the words of new songs or discussions. Can you relate to the lyrics, even if it's a genre of music that's unfamiliar to you? You can also download motivational speeches and audio books by your favorite speakers and authors.

Shop by yourself and go into different stores. Don't bring anyone along or ask for opinions on how you look. Trends and friends may have influenced how you dress, but what do *you* really like to wear? Buy yourself a brand-new outfit that's different from the rest of your wardrobe and admire how stunning you look in it. Observe your unique features and relish in your divine beauty.

Reward yourself more often. When you take the stairs instead of the elevator, take a second and say, "Good job!" to yourself. When you do the right thing instead of the easy thing, give yourself an extra spa day. Pamper yourself as all women love to do. Spend your day getting a massage and sauna, or at the nail or hair salon, or at a beauty lounge receiving a facial or skin treatment—whatever makes you feel good about yourself! And when you do slip up, don't be so hard on yourself. Contemplate on where you went wrong and how you can fix it. Write down your thoughts, intentions, and tentative solutions.

Engage in a hobby you've never tried before. The only time Alexandra painted was in an art class in elementary school, but recently she stepped into an arts and crafts store for something unrelated and happened to walk by the painting section. She was strangely drawn to a blank canvas for sale and decided, "Why not? Let me try it." She brought home her new possession, took out the brushes and colors, and began to paint. At first her intended masterpiece looked like stick figures, but as she layered the colors and filled in the spaces, Alexandra started feeling attached to her little work of art because it held meaning for her.

If you don't like the idea of painting, you can draw, write, sew, plant, meditate, dance, or anything that teaches your mind and body a brand-new skill. You can fix electronics if you feel like it, but the point is to disengage from your usual routine and have a go at a new craft that promotes creativity and emotional flow. We want you to notice that you can make yourself good at anything you put your mind to. We hope that you end up liking your new hobby so much that you'll continue it after your thirty days are over!

We also hope that during this month, you'll come to the realization that some people who don't contribute to your good might still be in your life, like the ex-partner who still calls you or the friend who's always judging you. Do you really need such influences? They are depreciating your value. If you can go thirty days without someone and not really miss them, you don't need them. Acknowledge also that other people's opinions should mean very little to you. How happy are you in your own company, without anyone to criticize, blame, or remind you of what you did wrong? You have no obstacles and no one to ruin your good mood! This is not to say that you'll kick everyone out of your life during this exercise but that you have the emotional intelligence to discern the true intentions of others.

If you do reach the conclusion that someone in your life isn't playing a positive role (especially an ex or guy who keeps contacting to you), here's an exercise to help you refrain from reaching out to him. When strong emotions surge, you might feel compelled to get them off your chest. Maybe you feel the need to say some things you didn't get to say to a former partner, share your final thoughts after an argument, or text a man who's bad news. When this need arises, stop yourself for just a moment. No matter how strongly the little voice in your head might be goading you to contact him, find the voice of logic instead. Write down what you want to say so that you release the emotions, but don't send the message. Stand in front of a mirror and say everything you'd say if you were face-to-face with him.

When you do go out with friends, suggest going somewhere you've never been before, such as a new restaurant, lounge, or club. You never know what great things can happen under the energy of a new environment!

And of course, buy a delicious ice cream and curl up with your favorite movies of all time to celebrate this newfound friendship with yourself.

At the culmination of these thirty self-filled days, you will experience a revelation. You will know what you want and absolutely don't want in a relationship, because you'll finally know yourself. Be confident in what you have learned about your wonderful, unique being. Know also that you deserve a partner who will encourage the authenticity you've now come to know and love.

THE POWER OF THE SPOKEN WORD

Before, during, and after your month-long detox, we encourage you to use affirmations for empowerment. Some people think that mantras are just New Age fluff. Not so. Chants, mantras, and affirmations have been around since human beings developed a system of speech. They were first used as a way of asking the universe for what we needed to survive: during a dry spell we chanted to bring on rain, and when the harvest was poor we intoned that crops would soon grow.

Repeated phrases were woven into the cultures and traditions of tribes all over the globe before modern societies formed. In Hinduism and Buddhism, a mantra is a sacred utterance that possesses a spiritual force behind it. Buddhists chant during meditation, and mantras are a part of initiation ceremonies in many Hindu sects. Music even evolved from chanting, which is why the verse and chorus of a song are repeated several times. Affirmations can be thought of as a form of prayer in the present tense, as if the things we're praying for are springing into life right now. Even in newer religions like Catholicism, what is a prayer but an affirmation of what we want God to grant us?

Words are responsible for everything you hold to be true. Why do you believe certain stories, customs, or traditions? Because someone told you to believe them. Growing up, your parents told you how to behave, your teachers taught you what you needed to learn, and the news announced what was going on in the world. The spoken word is responsible for how you think and act today.

Chances are that you recite mantras all the time without noticing. You tell yourself things every day, rarely recognizing the magnitude of your words and what you're affirming to be true. If you had a built-in tracker that automatically kept count of the phrases you spoke each day, you would be surprised at your choice of words. Out of habit, you might tell yourself, "I'm scared," "I'm tired," "I'm desperate," "I'm stuck," or, "I'm not good enough." What you might not realize is that your words form the truth of your life. What you keep thinking, you speak. What you keep speaking, you do. And what you keep doing, you attract.

A major step to changing your relationships is changing the way you relate to your problems and, by extension, the way you speak about them. When a problem arises, what words do you use to describe the situation? Do you tell others that you're "helpless" and a "victim"? You have to take control of the things that threaten to take control of you. You have to change "I'm weak" to "I'm powerful."

"I am" and "I can" are the single most important phrases you'll ever speak. That's because what follows these words sets up who you are: they determine what you believe, allow, and invite into your life. "I am" becomes even more profound when you redefine yourself throughout the day: "I am confident," "I am beautiful," and "I am loved" or "I am ready for love" are just a few of the countless declarations you can make to re-center your soul. "I can" will instantly replenish your power: "I can finish my workout," "I can attract a great lover," and "I can do this!" are all effective at giving you the boost of strength you need. Reciting the right words with purpose and conviction can shift your perception entirely. You will feel calm, at ease, and in control after speaking certain affirmations. You'll start to see things differently so that you can do things differently.

The key is to personalize your mantras so that they speak *to* you, not just for you. So instead of saying, "I am powerful," say, "I am powerful enough to overcome my breakup and attract a boyfriend who's loyal to me." Or instead of, "I can create a healthy relationship," say, "I can create a healthy relationship with Phil because we love each other."

"I PROMISE"

An affirmation is like a promise between you and the universe. When you make a promise, you send forth your intentions to become reality. You promise things to other people on a daily basis: you promise to be on time, take out the trash, and love your spouse 'til death do you part. Many promises are made, but few are kept. And that's okay, you should never take personally what another person wasn't able to deliver. At the end of the day, the promises that matter most are the ones you make—and keep!—to yourself.

The promises you make to yourself speak volumes about your level of commitment. If you want to enjoy healthy relationships with others, you have to be able to stick to the goals and limits you've set for your own good. We want you to wake up each day with a new promise to improve, one daily vow that will make you happier and healthier and serve you tomorrow. Pick your favorite phrases from the list below and repeat them throughout the day. They are vows that will strengthen your self-dedication. Choose the ones you have the most trouble believing and feel free to change them around. You will see that, with time, these empowering statements will come to you effortlessly.

I promise to honor my worth. The demands of daily life and your responsibilities to others can easily diminish your worth. In truth, you're worth more than you know. You deserve to be blessed with prosperity, great health, and incredible love, all of which you'll begin to attract the moment you promise to honor your worth.

I promise to make my intentions clear. Intentions are the starting point of any goal; they link conscious thought to bona fide action. Think of a few important things you need to accomplish soon, and organize your intentions in a clear, concise way, emphasizing the actions you'll take to bring them to life. Always make your intentions known to your partner to keep your relationship flowing smoothly.

I promise to educate myself. Education isn't limited to school or books. It implies learning about different beliefs, history, world events, and future concepts in whatever way works for you. All you have to do to learn is watch the world with vigilance. Knowledge endows you with an acceptance of the world as it was, is, and will be. As the Roman poet Virgil said, "Happy is he who has been able to learn the causes of things."

I promise to show more compassion. Compassion is our most neglected grace. It's easier to be aggressive than kind, so we respond with unnecessary aggression to everyday matters. But the solutions to problems are made possible through empathy and patience. Whether it's letting a car into your lane or recycling to save your environment, compassion takes many forms and often not more than a few minutes. Remember to extend compassion to yourself as well.

I promise to stand up for myself. At some point in life, you'll find yourself in situations that are quite unfair to you. Stand up for yourself in a polite but firm way. Defending your rights demands respect from others. Don't be afraid to voice your opinion and seek justice for yourself. Because if you don't stand up for yourself, who will?

I promise to finish what I start. Leaving a goal halfway finished means you'll never know what could've happened if you had completed it. As difficult as it may be, there's nothing more rewarding than doing something the right way, through effort and ambition. Practice discipline to meet the finish line.

I promise to evolve. Evolution is the first law of the universe: what does not evolve dies out. We too must shift and change, little by little, day by day. Promise to yourself to become better. It can be as simple as taking up a yoga routine or ending a long-standing feud. Through honest introspection, you'll realize in what areas of life you need to advance.

I promise to end negative patterns. Patterns keep us stagnant and stuck. Often we can become trapped in a bad situation without even knowing it. From a series of similar relationships to dead-end jobs to making the wrong choices, all patterns can be broken by modifying your behavior. To end the repetition of negative cycles, you have to take new actions that yield new results. Chapter 3 laid out the steps to do this.

I promise not to let others to affect me. Realize that your happiness is in your hands; you hold the key to unwavering joy. When your mood is compromised, go within yourself and restabilize your emotions. Affirm to yourself that no one can harm you. Say, "I am the keeper of my joy, which is whole, unhurt, and intact."

I promise to take nothing for granted. We've all heard the phrase, "You don't know what you've got until it's gone," but not until we lose something or someone special do these words really hit home. Then, our sadness lies in remembrance; we question why we didn't appreciate a person or period in our lives. Promise to take nothing for granted again and enjoy everything while you have the chance. Wrap yourself in tender moments, adding a tight embrace or a long kiss to your list of cherished memories. As tiny or fleeting as these actions may be, they are yours.

A promise is your word of honor. Before you make another promise to anyone else, pledge these ten statements to yourself. They will solidify your self-worth and strengthen your devotion to yourself.

EVERYDAY COMMITMENT

To help you become more comfortable with the idea of committing to a relationship, start by committing to something that betters you on a daily basis. Dedicate yourself to one special task each day, whether it's a new class, book, exercise routine, or volunteer work. Take it up as if it were part of you, immersing yourself in it and becoming intimate with it. When you feel you've executed this commitment to its highest potential, stop and undertake a new one. The key is to continue committing yourself to things that help you evolve.

Many people find it hard to stick to a daily commitment because their approach is disorganized. You have to plan ahead of time to exercise or work on your project or finish writing your song. Set adequate time aside for your activity, at least one hour a day. Do it during the hour of the day when you're most alert and energetic, whether that's morning or evening for you. Prepare yourself mentally by reminding yourself how much you enjoy doing this activity and the benefits it brings to your mind, body, and spirit.

You may already be completely committed to your child or your pet, or you may be a caretaker for a parent or family member who's ill. If so, examine how you're approaching these challenging tasks. The ways in which your child tests your patience may also be the ways in which your partner tests your patience: talking back to you, not paying attention, or not doing what you ask. The things your family member does that frustrate you may be the same things your partner does that frustrate you. It's essential that you work on improving your current commitments so that you're better equipped to handle commitment in a love relationship.

VISUALIZATION FOR COMMITMENT

Your mind's eye is the fertile ground where the seeds of reality are planted. If you're not in an ideal relationship right now (or you're not in a relationship at all), you can begin to change this by choosing to see your situation differently.

Start with a simple thought that makes you happy and include either your current or prospective partner. It could be holding hands, sharing a laugh, kissing passionately, walking in a park, etc. Close your eyes and see it, registering every detail in your mind. But don't get too far into the daydream—one image is enough for one day.

The next day, continue with your visualization. What else do you see yourself and your partner doing? Have you left the park, and are you going to dinner now? Is he saying anything to you?

Pick up this visualization every day, starting from the beginning and moving through various scenes with your loved one. See it intently, purposefully, and joyfully. Visualize an ideal day with your significant other until the day it becomes a reality.

Chapter 5

COMMITMENT THROUGH THE SEVEN ARCHETYPES

You are the manifestation of an archetype
set into the universe long ago.
—Carmen Harra

WHAT ARE ARCHETYPES?

Throughout history, we've tried to classify people into different groups according to their personalities in an attempt to understand "why they do the things they do." This is the basis for all psychology. Why does one person lie and another tell the truth? Why does one person cheat and another remain faithful?

The word *archetype* comes from the Greek *archein*, meaning "original," and *typos*, meaning "pattern." So an archetype is an original pattern. In psychology, it's a pattern of thought present in the human psyche.

The forerunner of prototypes was Plato's theory of forms, his argument being that all forms (things) on Earth draw their origins from perfect forms in the realm of ideals. According to this theory, the patterns we perceive in our world are merely representations of a perfect pattern on some higher plane of existence.

Carl Jung was inspired by Plato's forms and applied the concept to human psychology. Jung believed that universal patterns reside within the depths of our consciousness and surface in the form of beliefs, fears, wishes, and so on. He identified three basic human motivations—the Ego, the Self, and the Soul—containing four archetypes each. The Ego is made up of the Innocent, the Orphan, the Hero, and the Caregiver. The Soul is comprised of the Explorer, the Rebel, the Lover, and the Creator. The Self is represented through the Jester, the Sage, the Magician, and the Ruler. Each of these twelve archetypes is the human incarnation of an ideal form. We share the Jungian belief that archetypes are manifestations of the collective consciousness which we experience throughout life.

"What is the evidence that archetypes exist?" you might ask. Well, one way we know archetypes exist is our very own evolution. Humans derive from an original mold of their kind. If we analyze the forces that drive us, we will see that they're mutual throughout the human race: we run on the same thread. We all strive for ideals of love, liberty, and happiness, among others. We know an archetype for the concept of love exists because love is ingrained in us, even if it's intangible or has innumerable definitions. We continue to draw on cosmic consciousness—thinking, feeling, and doing the same things that have existed since the dawn of time. Archetypes are nestled within the very roots of our nature. We cannot change them; we can only change how we relate to them as we expand our understanding.

The theory of archetypes can be well applied to relationships. The ways in which we relate (or don't relate) to another person also emerge from our subconscious. We have witnessed this truth for many years, working as psychologists and intuitive counselors and hearing every type of love scenario imaginable. We've worked with women who desperately desired the emotionally unavailable man, women who sought to escape the overwhelming man, couples that fell out of love then back in love, and men who realized they had been living a lie and actually loved other men. You name it, we've heard it.

CARMEN HARRA, PH.D. AND ALEXANDRA HARRA

In listening to tens of thousands of cases over time, something interesting happened: we noticed that the same *types* of people kept cropping up—people unrelated to each other but displaying almost identical qualities and comportment. As soon as a client started describing the man she was dating, we could almost finish her sentence, because we knew what came next based on the archetype she was describing.

We began to comprehend that personality traits descend from archetypes and that a person's very behavior is steered by his higher design. We noted that people come with sets of characteristics, similar to how a person with red hair also has freckles or a person with dark skin usually has dark eyes. For example, someone who is predisposed to introversion is also likely to have issues with communication and trust. We also realized that while we inherit much of our personality, it's not fully formed until we pass through experiences that solidify who we are. No one is born narcissistic or too independent, addicted to his work or to the idea of love, emotionally reserved or wounded. But the likelihood for someone to become introverted will be exacerbated if that person is bullied in school, not shown enough love at home, or rejected by a lover.

We believe a person's archetype is encoded in his genes, even if it's not physically apparent. It continues to develop through his early relationship with his family and incipient awareness of his sexuality. The latter is dependent on the former: a person's relationship with his family during his youth sets the groundwork for his relationship with his sexuality as he enters adulthood. A mother's or father's parenting style will impact the child for life, long after he moves out of the house.

Karina is a family friend whom we've known for a long time. We've been witness to Karina's struggles during every stage of her life; she had a very domineering mother who just wouldn't give her any freedom, even after she grew up. Karina was accompanied everywhere by her mom, who felt the need to drop her off and pick her up from work. Karina had to respect a curfew even in her mid-twenties, and she wasn't allowed to date because according to Karina's mother, no one was good enough to be with her little girl.

Those who knew Karina made fun of her mother's overprotectiveness, but it was no laughing matter; it took a serious toll on Karina's life. She never matured into a real woman as a result. At thirty, Karina was still socially awkward and had trouble being with a man, remaining dutiful to her mother for as long as she was alive.

In another noteworthy case, Joey's mother never taught him the importance of caring for his home. She was in charge of cooking, cleaning, raising Joey and his siblings, and maintaining the household. Joey's father went to work and brought home money, but not much else. When it was time for him to start his own family, Joey repeated what he had witnessed growing up, mimicking the role his father had held in his house. Joey's mother had gotten married in her late teens and Joey got married in his late teens. His mom had been a homemaker who answered to her husband's commands, and Joey fully expected his new wife to do as such.

To Joey's great surprise, his wife resisted many of his demands and required him to participate in running their household. Joey laughed at his wife's request to change their newborn's diapers, stating that this was "the woman's job." Needless to say, this couple didn't last very long. Joey's mother probably thought she was doing him a favor by not burdening him with household chores, but she had actually done her son a great disservice that would lead to the end of his marriage. Karina and Joey serve as striking examples of how our relationship with our parents shapes both our archetype and love life.

A few years ago, someone advised Alexandra to write a book for young women on how to recognize Mr. Right from Mr. Wrong. When we talked about this, we realized it's not quite that easy. While it's true that some partners are just plain wrong for us, most human beings are far more complex than we can imagine. Our characters aren't black or white, good or bad; we are a symphony of colors. Our personalities are multidimensional. It is, therefore, not our place to tell you that the archetype you're dating or would like to date is right or wrong for you. We're here to provide insight into what you can expect. The value of the seven archetypes we've identified is that they serve as a predictability chart, laying out all the components of a man's personality. We present each archetype's most critical character traits—innate and learned—that influence his relationships positively and negatively.

A CLOSER LOOK AT THE SEVEN ARCHETYPES

We continued observing the personas we encountered in our practice, particularly in regard to how they handled love relationships. We began taking notes on our clients' backgrounds, experiences, and demeanors and eventually developed seven distinct archetypes:

1. The Independent
2. The Workaholic
3. The Narcissist
4. The Free Spirit
5. The Hopeless Romantic
6. The Wounded Warrior
7. The Introvert

More specifically, we divided the archetypes into two categories: the "me" archetypes and the "we" archetypes. The difference between the two is how much the archetype relies on his ego to make decisions in his relationships. The Independent, the Workaholic, the Narcissist, and the Free Spirit are more ego driven, while the Hopeless Romantic, the Wounded Warrior, and the Introvert employ their egos less. Selfishness or selflessness will impact the energy of a relationship tremendously. We also provide an analysis of the truly balanced individual, which we call the Well-Rounded One, in comparison to the other archetypes. Our next two chapters focus on the archetypes within these categories.

Each of the seven archetypes possesses strengths and weaknesses, and each is capable of upholding a relationship so long as he's willing to work on himself. As stated before, we believe there's no such thing as a commitment-phobe, but some archetypes adapt to commitment more easily than others: certain attributes lend them a higher susceptibility to attachment and a keener sense of dedication. Other archetypes are more emotionally resistant or have tougher psychological barriers to overcome before they can engage in a healthy relationship.

It boils down to what *values* each archetype must learn or change in order to cultivate a relationship that's fulfilling for both partners. For example, the Narcissist needs to learn the value of sacrifice. The Independent needs to learn the value of attachment. The Workaholic needs to learn to prioritize what really matters, the Wounded Warrior needs to heal, and the Free Spirit needs to ground himself in purpose. The Hopeless Romantic needs to be more realistic, while the Introvert needs to open up and trust.

It's key to understand that our archetypes are not indicative of disorders. They might shed light on someone's temperament or the ways in which that person is likely to respond to commitment, but that doesn't necessarily mean any of the archetypes suffer from a social or personality disorder. While the Narcissist is more prone to narcissistic personality disorder, our version most likely doesn't have NPD. And although he's been hurt in his past, a Wounded Warrior doesn't have to have post-traumatic stress disorder. Some people do develop personality disorders for various reasons, but they're not always correlated to their archetype: The Free Spirit can appear extroverted and fun, but on the inside, he could be battling an avoidant personality disorder. Our archetypes are, therefore, not a diagnosis for any individual illness or disorder. Only by interacting with a patient one-on-one are we able to make that distinction.

Each archetype needs to unlearn something unhealthy or unhelpful, then learn something new and positive, to be in a successful relationship. We don't want to remain confined to the limitations of our archetype, unable to live up to our commitment goals and reneging on our promises. This causes us much suffering and confusion, not to mention a heck of a lot of trouble for our partner! Our goal is to escape the boundaries of one archetype and become as flexible as possible in our lives and our romances, ready to tackle any challenge. The goal isn't to achieve perfection but balance.

THE ARCHETYPES IN A FEW WORDS

The Independent

The Independent's struggle with commitment is caused by his individualistic and detached nature. Of the seven archetypes, the Independent is most reluctant to enter a relationship because he fears a partner will compromise his cherished freedom. The Independent is defined by his need to be on his own, and this becomes true not only in his love relationships but many other areas of his life. The Independent doesn't look to what others are doing; he forges his own path.

The Workaholic

The Workaholic has built his life around his work. In fact, he chose his career long before he chose his significant other. But he still wants the best of both worlds—the successful job and the beautiful wife—and he isn't willing to compromise. Under no circumstances can the Workaholic be with a stultifying, possessive woman who holds him back from carrying out his mission; his partner will have to be supportive of his career and responsibilities. He sees the woman who's constantly on top of him as another liability, not an asset that adds to his life. The Workaholic will let go of the partner who's not contributing to his growth in the same way he'll fire an employee who's not performing up to his expectations.

The Narcissist

The Narcissist has crossed the boundary from empowerment to entitlement, where there is too little humility and too much hubris. His heightened ego and selfish inclinations preclude him from bonding fully with others, which can make him seem emotionally superficial and cause serious relationship problems. The Narcissist may have trouble paying enough attention to his partner or giving her what she needs because his focus is so often on himself. But if these character tendencies are mitigated, the Narcissist can commit to a relationship.

The Free Spirit

This archetype is undecided in all that he does: from relationships to work to hobbies, the Free Spirit has trouble sticking to commitment in multiple aspects of his life. This man may claim he wants to have a relationship but abandons ship when things get serious. This kind of irrational behavior can leave his partner bemused and blaming herself when in reality, the Free Spirit contends with the notion of commitment itself. Unlike the Independent, who's afraid of losing himself to his partner, the Free Spirit simply doesn't know what he wants. He may have a faint idea, but when thinking comes to doing, the Free Spirit can't execute. To teach him to pull through, you'll first have to help the Free Spirit find his authentic self and act on it.

The Hopeless Romantic

The Hopeless Romantic is an idealist of epic proportions. He whole-heartedly believes in love but is a bit aimless and tactless. A dreamer and not a doer, the Hopeless Romantic yearns for commitment but doesn't know how to approach a relationship in a rational and clear-sighted way. He falls in love easily, throwing himself into romances blindly and often with unsuitable women. In truth, he may be more in love with the *idea* of love than with the person in front of him. Because he idealizes love, he's not realistic about the messiness that relationships bring.

The Wounded Warrior

Because he's been wounded (possibly early in life), the Wounded Warrior experiences a disconnection between the outside and the inside: the smile he wears without doesn't match the turmoil he feels within. The Wounded Warrior is dealing with demons that he not only doesn't address but willfully suppresses. He tries to hide or mask his trauma, often unsuccessfully, until it suddenly boils to the surface. Before he can commit, the Wounded Warrior must gently explore and heal his sunken pain.

The Introvert

The Introvert's struggle is his fear of intimacy and hesitation to release what he feels inside. His bane is his lack of communication, which can be misinterpreted by his partner as secrecy. There exists a discrepancy between what's shown on the outside and what's kept inside that's unique to the Introvert. To be in a committed relationship, the Introvert needs to feel comfortable enough to open himself up to his partner.

After you read about the seven different archetypes and decide which one applies to your significant other, we offer you a description of the Well-Rounded One. The Well-Rounded One is not an archetype per say, but he paints the portrait of a truly stable partner. Through him, you'll understand how a healthy relationship looks and feels. The ultimate goal is that, once you and your partner have performed your work, you'll shed the encumbrances of your archetypes and become a well-rounded couple.

YOU ARE WHAT YOU FEEL

In reading this book you may wonder, *How do I identify my and my partner's archetype?* By observing your emotions and actions, as well as his, for a certain amount of time. Each day you're on a roller coaster of emotions that can shift quite suddenly: one moment life couldn't be better; the next moment life is an absolute mess. Fluctuating feelings are normal, but sometimes we can't seem to get off this ride. Despite this stream of conflictual feelings, we experience a few emotions most often throughout the day. It is these dominant emotions that allow us to pinpoint our archetype. Let's identify and do a little work with them.

Your journey to emotional and physical health begins by deciphering the feelings that govern you. Before anything else, you must accept how you're feeling at any given moment because your emotions are a part of you; they come from you and no one else. Whether it's contempt or mistrust, you can use this knowledge to identify which archetype you fit right now while simultaneously working to elevate what you feel every day.

The first key is knowing your triggers. You encourage positive emotions when you avoid situations and cut off people that bring out the "bad" in you. Don't apologize for distancing yourself from friends or family who stir up stress in your life, events that make you anxious, and memories that plague you with guilt. Failure to do so may result in emotional imbalances that affect other areas of your life, especially love relationships.

Again, the more your brain senses one type of emotion, the more likely that it will become your dominant emotion, the default mood that dictates your personality. If you become frustrated over every little obstacle that pops up, you'll live in constant frustration. If you're angry at the world every day, you're sending a message to your brain to produce more anger. Anger is our most stubborn emotion; it rarely wants to let us go. Over time, you might find yourself feeling dark emotions over negligible things: a long line at checkout, a tire low on air, etc. When we have no patience for anything, negative feelings take over quickly. Our emotions can become as addictive as any drug.

To interrupt this series of adverse emotions and conquer the disadvantages of your archetype, you will need to rewire the nerve cells in your brain. Human beings are unique in that we have an incredible ability to transmute our emotions, to take a feeling and change it into a more productive and enlightening one. So denial can evolve into acceptance. Hate can be transmuted into love. Disinterest can be switched into motivation. Doubt can be converted into faith. If you frequently experience negative emotions, you can choose to gently transition out of them. The best way is to shift away from the negative emotion when it arises: if you feel yourself becoming frustrated, *stop* the emotion. Yes, you can stop an emotion through certain strategies. Oftentimes, the solution might be simply to apply logic.

Reasoning through your feelings can help you differentiate between rational and irrational emotions and disassociate yourself from unhealthy ones like fear, worry, and anger. For example, it's rational to feel disappointed for being fired from your job but irrational to feel disappointed *in yourself* if it wasn't your fault. Remember that harboring such emotions hurts no one but you and that it's always in your best interests to release feelings that don't contribute to your mental, emotional, and physical growth. If you do this enough times, your brain's preoccupation will diminish altogether. Blocking a recurring feeling as soon as it starts to simmer will help you react differently to stressful situations over time. It can take several weeks to adjust to new emotions because the human brain likes to follow predictable patterns of thought, even if they aren't the healthiest.

As long as you remain in denial about your feelings and don't confront them candidly, you can't hope to surpass them. We're all vulnerable to the people we love and sensitive to the ups and downs of life. Once you accept this, you can begin to address the emotional propensities of your archetype.

In the following exercise, you're going to identify your dominant emotions. This will not only lay the groundwork for identifying your archetype, it will teach you how to convert your primary emotion (especially if it's harmful or self-limiting) into a more positive feeling. The emotions we feel on a daily basis shape our personalities; we take the actions we take because of the way we feel at that moment. It is therefore essential that you not only understand but befriend the emotion you experience most.

Keep a journal of your emotions for one week. As soon as you wake up, write the date at the top of the page and your first emotion of the day. Then throughout the day, scribble down any strong emotions that surge. This can be anything from annoyance to excitement to anxiety. Try to go deeper than "happy" or "sad." Next to the emotion also note the cause. Remain aware of what you're feeling throughout the day, especially when you interact with your loved one. What emotions does he evoke in you? With what emotions do you respond to him?

Note also how you're reacting when such feelings come up. When you're irritated, do you take it out on people who didn't do anything to deserve it? When you're nostalgic, do you retreat and close yourself off to the people who care about you? We're all visited by negative emotions, but we should never let these guests become permanent residents. Recognizing that all emotions are normal will help you return to a positive state of mind more quickly. It's important not to dwell on negative feelings so as to encourage emotional flow and avoid stagnancy. What we choose to do with our emotions—whether we choose to diffuse them through healthy outlets, bury them deep within us, or unleash them on unsuspecting victims—has a sizeable impact on our relationships.

After you've completed the exercise, reflect on your journal entries to locate your dominant emotion. Can you make a clear link between that emotion and one of the archetypes? Is it fear of failure? Personal ambition that disregards others? Apprehension at the thought of becoming vulnerable? Then it's clear what your archetype might be.

If you're not sure, repeat the exercise for a few more days. Keep a record of your most prevalent feelings and reactions. Do you see a connection to one of the archetypes? If you can't identify a strong enough emotion or you don't notice a lot of negative feelings, you may be a Well-Rounded Man or Woman, which is the model we should all strive to become.

It can be tricky to detect your archetype based on your emotions because you can have conflicting personality traits: you can be shy like an Introvert under some circumstances yet outgoing like an Independent under others. We're capable of producing a wide range of emotions, which can be confusing in determining our character. Some emotions can also pertain to more than one archetype; you can be closed off as a result of natural introversion or inner wounds—two very different reasons. As a rule of thumb, what you feel on a daily basis will reveal your main archetype, but that doesn't mean you can't have a second, recessive archetype. You can be an Independent with a tendency to overwork yourself like a Workaholic, for instance, or a Free Spirit with a strong ego like the Narcissist. Understanding what emotions you feel most powerfully, as well as what actions they lead you to take, will shed light on your prevailing personality type.

This exercise can catch you off guard. You might be seriously surprised by the emotions you experience and act on every day, especially if they're feelings that float up from your subconscious without awareness. You might ask yourself, "Why do I keep getting mad over the smallest things?" or, "Why do I run out of patience so quickly?" There's a reason for that, and discovering it will help you better manage your feelings.

Maybe in trying to identify your dominant emotion, you discover that you're an archetype you don't want to be. Few people want to admit that they're selfish or carry around trauma from their past. So maybe you'll think, *Oh my god, I'm a Narcissist!* or, *Wow, I'm a Wounded Warrior. I've been living in my past.* Our response is, *so what?* So what if you're a Narcissist or a Wounded Warrior or a Hopeless Romantic who gave her heart away to the wrong guy? Accepting your archetype is tantamount to accepting yourself. This is who you are right now, but it doesn't have to be who you will be tomorrow. All you need to become the best version of you is desire to improve. Making peace with your emotions, no matter how disconcerting or disorganized they may be, is the first step to transforming them.

We both tried this exercise and were taken aback by our results. I, Carmen, turned out to be a Well-Rounded Woman, owing to my pragmatism and solution-seeking nature as well as my long-standing marriage to my late husband, whom I identified as having been a Wounded Warrior. Alexandra ended up being an Introvert; although she doesn't mind being in the limelight, she prefers working with her creativity behind the scenes. Alexandra also found that she doesn't unveil much of her personality to others until after they've earned her trust.

You can follow this same approach to narrow down the archetype of a potential love interest. Observe him closely during your encounters. What dominant emotion does he display? What themes continually surface in his conversations (not just with you, but ones you may overhear while he's on the phone or talking to someone else)? What does your intuition tell you about the person? This is not a foolproof method, but it can provide you with insight, over time, about the archetype guiding your significant other.

AT HIS WORST AND BEST

From worst to best, our emotions constitute our nature. Similarly, each archetype operates on several core emotions that form the basis of who he is. These descriptions may further help you identify your partner's archetype:

At his worst, the Independent operates on stubbornness, detachment, and disinterest. At his best, he operates on receptivity, responsibility, and reliability.

At his worst, the Workaholic operates on insatiability, ambition, and avarice. At his best, he operates on charity, modesty, and simplicity.

At his worst, the Narcissist operates on intimidation, insolence, and self-infatuation. At his best, he operates on altruism, empathy, and sacrifice.

At his worst, the Free Spirit operates on unconventionality, carelessness, and disorientation. At his best, he operates on purpose, diligence, and practicality.

At his worst, the Hopeless Romantic operates on idealism, recklessness, and self-sacrifice. At his best, he operates on logic, balance, and healthy limits.

At his worst, the Wounded Warrior operates on regret, pain, and self-sabotage. At his best, he operates on hope, forgiveness, and resilience.

At his worst, the Introvert operates on isolation, overthinking, and reservation. At his best, he operates on creativity, sharing, and confidence.

Chapter 6

THE "ME" ARCHETYPES: THE INDEPENDENT, THE WORKAHOLIC, THE NARCISSIST, AND THE FREE SPIRIT

THE INDEPENDENT

The Independent is afraid of losing himself to his partner.
—Alexandra Harra

The Independent is one of the more reluctant archetypes to enter into a relationship because he treasures his freedom. The Independent is defined by a need to be on his own, and this holds true not only in his love relationship but in the way he works: he performs well in positions that allow him to work for himself or by himself, being well-organized, disciplined, and focused on progress. The Independent doesn't look at what others are doing; he carves his own path through life.

His Independent aptitude is evident from early on. Even as a child, the Independent might have taken his toys and went to play on his own. In many cases, one or both parents stressed this was the "right" way to be; the Independent's autonomy is psychologically linked to notions of success and happiness that were imparted on him in childhood. Unlike the Free Spirit, who experiences commitment problems on a broader spectrum, the Independent has issues committing to a love relationship in particular.

The Independent doesn't necessarily come across as romantic or emotional. He doesn't want to get a phone call from his girlfriend crying her heart out because he won't really know what to say to comfort her, although he has good intentions and wants to help her feel better. The Independent may not always feel as deeply as others do. He experiences a psychological gap at the level of bonding with another human being, especially in the sense of emotional intimacy. The Independent associates strong emotional attachment with commitment that he believes is beyond his capacity.

This type of man controls his feelings well and he doesn't let his weaknesses show in any sense of the word. Of the archetypes, Independents are closest to being masters over their emotions. When you first meet him, the Independent comes across as engaging, approachable, and sociable, which makes you like him. But after you start to get to know him, he can turn cold, tough, and hard to reach, which, ironically, some women swoon over!

The Independent erects boundaries that a woman can't cross. He'll let her come close while still keeping her at arm's length. From not letting his partner into his personal space to subconsciously sabotaging potential relationships, the Independent has built emotional walls around himself. The moment a woman starts chipping away at these walls and breaches his boundaries, the Independent's flight response kicks in, fear suddenly sweeps over him, and he recalls how much he loves his independence.

The Independent values his own abilities more than he values partnership—what he can do for himself over what others can do for him. He's so concerned with meeting his own needs that he can't see someone else fulfilling them. He is needy, like everyone else, but he either believes a woman can't meet his needs or that she'll strip him of his identity if she does. The Independent feels that he's worked hard to preserve this lifestyle and that commitment comes at a serious price. He lives well on his own and stands on his own two feet, running his household by himself, cooking for himself, and making his own appointments. He comes and goes as he pleases, and to the

Independent, that sort of freedom is priceless. However, he does realize that he *should* be in a relationship. At times he might even think there's something wrong with him for not being married by now.

This fits the description of a client named Roy, who didn't want to compromise his lifestyle but simultaneously felt the need to commit to a woman. He was worried that he might be a commitment-phobe, but he also didn't want to forfeit what he enjoyed doing on a daily basis, like going out with his buddies or spending hours in the gym. Roy led a normal life outside of the fact that he couldn't keep up a relationship; he had a great career and solid friendships.

Roy came to us a good number of times expressing his desire for a relationship. Each time he walked into our office, he was excited about a new girl he had recently met. Roy would tell us all about his budding love interest, even showing us photos and recounting the details of their last date. But when we asked Roy where he saw this going, he would stay quiet. In his mind, Roy wasn't sure what, if anything, would develop out of his brand-new romance because thinking too far into the future scared him. The potential for things to become serious pushed Roy back to square one.

The next time Roy came for a session, it was to deliver the unfortunate news that he was no longer seeing the woman he had been so excited about. He stated that she had come on too strong and too fast. Roy now described a new hopeful candidate (who also didn't last long), and the cycle continued. What often ends up being the case with the Independent is that he starts to like a woman—even like her a lot—but then some small thing she does turns him off completely. He then remembers how much he likes being on his own and reverts to old habits.

Tony was a more serious case of the Independent than Roy, as Tony didn't feel the need to commit. His way of thinking was, *Why tie myself down if I don't have to?* He dated girls here and there, had fun and traveled with them, without ever giving them the impression that they were getting into a relationship. Tony never passed on an opportunity but also never gave a woman the opportunity to be with him. Similar to a Free Spirit, his independence transcended love relationships: Tony had an overall detached personality in every respect of the word. He floated from job to job and ended up working as a freelance web designer at his own leisure. He joined the gym, quit, and then joined again. He saw his family then went years without seeing them. Even outside of his relationships, Tony couldn't fully commit. Some Independents can border on Free Spirits if their commitment problems extend into other areas of life.

Misconceptions about the Independent: Many women interpret the Independent's conduct as outright rejection. And since it's human nature to crave what we can't have, some women then make it their life mission to get his attention; they swear that they'll be the ones to get an Independent to change and commit. This is not the right mentality or approach to have with this archetype, not to mention that it's utterly ineffective. *The Independent likes to chase, not be chased.* You'll have to have realistic expectations about how far you can get with an Independent and in what frame of time. Some men in this archetype can conquer their commitment barriers completely and some only partially. Then there are men who remain independent for as long as they live but they've found partners who are able to tolerate them as they are. Don't draw any conclusions about your own Independent love interest until you can measure some progress.

How he really thinks: The Independent can be pretty introverted in his thoughts and ambitions, choosing not to share what he thinks or wants all the time. But what distinguishes him from an actual Introvert is that he has no problem being the center of attention. He isn't affected by crowds, noise, or parties like a true Introvert. The Independent lives in the paradox of being immensely confident in himself yet highly insecure about sharing his life with someone. On the outside, he comes across as charismatic and ready to win over a woman. But on the inside, he feels he can't cope with the demands of a relationship or the needs of another human being. The way he presents himself is inconsistent with the way he thinks.

The Independent has toyed with the idea of getting into a real relationship in his mind, but the murky waters of commitment pose too great a threat to his independence. He may even have attempted to get into serious relationships in the past, often with disastrous results. Thus he regresses to playing it safe and being on his own. But in his heart, the Independent both realizes he can't stay single forever and doesn't want to be alone. He'd like to be in a relationship, but with a woman who's easygoing and highly independent herself.

Can he commit? This type of man can offer commitment if there is patience and understanding on your part. If you believe your own Independent is worth the effort, you can take the right actions to get him to become ever-so-slowly attached to you.

Brian and Michelle were coworkers at Morgan Stanley. Brian seemed to really like Michelle, always striking up conversation with her during breaks. Brian also seemed to be single, never bringing up the subject of a wife or girlfriend. Michelle was enthusiastic about the prospect of seeing Brian outside of work and even thought he might be the right partner for her. So she worked up the nerve to ask Brian out and they went on a few casual dates.

After that, Michelle tried to get closer to Brian, contacting him more frequently and initiating conversation regularly. But Brian refused to let Michelle get too far into his world. He did go out with her, but he didn't reveal personal details about himself, never invited her to come over, and was careful not to let their conversations become too deep. Something inside Brian was walled up. Michelle counteracted Brian's inaccessibility by pushing even harder, certain she could break through. She took the liberty to buy Brian a shirt from a store he'd mentioned he liked and even brought him a home-cooked meal for lunch one day at work. But Michelle's good intentions backfired on her, and it became more and more difficult to see Brian outside of work after that. Michelle noticed that, ironically, Brian had plenty of friends and had no problems going out with them every other night, so why not with her? Michelle became desperate and released her frustrations on Brian, which only made him remove himself more. The more she stepped forward, it seemed, the further he backed away.

Michelle then came to us seeking guidance on how to make Brian come to her. She described Brian's behavior and we recognized him as the Independent archetype right away. We first advised her not to contact him anymore and to let communication come from him. Michelle did just that and it took Brian about a week to send her a text. He asked to see her, but we suggested that she politely decline his first attempt. This showed Brian that Michelle wasn't "needy" of him in any way. Michelle's refusal sparked more interest from Brian; perhaps she wasn't a clingy woman after all.

Brian contacted Michelle again and this time, she accepted his invitation. Over dinner, Michelle didn't ask probing questions or try to pry into Brian's private life like she had done on previous occasions. She didn't stress the frustration she felt from Brian's unresponsiveness. Instead, Michelle focused on the positive things they shared in common: they both enjoyed their work, fine wines, and cooking new recipes. The conversation flowed smoothly, and Brian was becoming more comfortable.

After a few more enjoyable dates, Brian confessed that he had needed some time to reach the conclusion that he felt better with Michelle than without her. He stated that he had a personal problem with being pressured but that he no longer felt pressured by her. Now that Michelle understood Brian's character, she was much less likely to flip out if he didn't call her for half a day or even if he needed a couple of days to himself. Michelle no longer felt driven to desperation by Brian's autonomy because she now had a handle on his way of thinking and being. Since then, the couple has been making small but significant strides toward commitment. The story of Brian and Michelle shows us that the Independent *can* commit, especially if he's found a woman who gets him.

What he needs from you: The Independent needs a woman who's able to give him his space. He does not want to hear you beg to see him or lay out the obvious logic of why you should spend more time together. He wants you to keep busy and tend to your own needs. The more you're able to do that, the more he'll come to you of his own accord.

You'll have to take baby steps toward commitment with the Independent. Coming on too strongly will make him run away with the speed of light, right back into his man cave. Don't try to barge into the Independent's life and start doing his laundry or making him breakfast. You might consider these nice gestures, but he'll consider them an invasion of privacy because he's used to doing things for himself a certain way. Communication is key with the Independent; ask him often what he wants or needs from you. If the answer is "nothing," then he really doesn't want you to do anything. But if the answer is to go to dinner, to come over, or to go to the movies, you're making progress. Let things come from the Independent. It's okay to contact him, but let him initiate conversation often. With time, the Independent should become steadily more committed to you as he realizes what a wonderful addition you are to his life.

Compatibility with the Independent: The Independent is most compatible with another Independent and with the Workaholic. A Mr. and Mrs. Independent make a great match; each will go about his or her business and neither will suffocate the other. Two Independents won't overwhelm each other with demands, and the Workaholic will be so wrapped up in her own work that that she'll give the Independent all the room he needs to be himself.

The Independent is least compatible with the Wounded Warrior and the Introvert. He won't be able to dedicate himself to the arduous task of helping the Wounded Warrior heal. And as the Independent is generally extroverted, he won't take the time to dissect the complexities of an Introvert.

Differences between male and female Independents: Men are more independent than women to begin with. A man can become even more independent when he's afraid of "losing himself" in a relationship or values his self-governing lifestyle too much to give it up. By nature, women are not Independents that evade relationships. Only recently did women start to become sovereign in this sense. There has been an enormous shift in the role of women in society in the last forty years and, consequently, in their relationships with men. As more and more women take positions of power and sustain themselves financially, they no longer rely on their male counterparts as they once did. Their mentality switched from dependent to independent as they underwent an awakening of their autonomy. A woman usually adopts an independent mentality after she learns (either through firsthand experience or the experiences of other women) that she shouldn't give up her sense of self in a relationship. Her emotions can harden from tough lessons in love.

Identifying qualities: Autonomous, self-reliant, needs personal space, outgoing, fearless, confident, detached, strong-willed, stoic, down-to-earth, practical, street smart, easily turned off, and has difficulty communicating.

Represented by: The eagle. Like the eagle, the Independent soars to great heights alone. He is equipped with a keen vision for his life and doesn't want to lose his tenacity and personal power to a partner.

Real-life Independents: Leonardo DiCaprio, Oprah Winfrey, and Rihanna.

THE WORKAHOLIC

The Workaholic's career is inseparable
from his relationships.
—Carmen Harra

The Workaholic has built his kingdom around his work, integrating his career into his life. It is an indivisible component of his identity in which he takes great pride. In fact, he chose his career long before he chose his significant other; so when a woman does come into his life, she'll have to be supportive of his work. Even after he retires (which he will do very reluctantly), the Workaholic will continue partaking in his work in one way or another.

The man in this category wants the best of both worlds and he's not willing to compromise: he wants the successful job *and* the beautiful wife. He is nearly addicted to his work because it allows him to express himself and gives him freedom to evolve. Under no circumstances can the Workaholic be with a stultifying, possessive woman who holds him back from fulfilling his vocation. He sees the woman who's constantly on top of him as a burden, not a joy. And he'll let go of a partner who's not contributing to his growth in the same way he'll fire an employee who's not performing up to his expectations.

The Workaholic is captivated by the woman who labors to advance her career and keeps just as busy as he does. Two bosses hard at work make one heck of a team! Although two Workaholics function well together, the female Workaholic doesn't have much time to cater to her husband, which can pose a problem since the male Workaholic needs all the help he can get from his companion. Because of this, the Workaholic usually ends up with the opposite: a housewife.

The Workaholic is a no-nonsense kind of man who abides by a mind-over-matter mentality. Seeing is believing to the Workaholic, who considers words without actions little more than false promises. This is an admirably ambitious individual who believes in his powers and skills. He has an optimistic attitude and is certain he can achieve anything he wants. The Workaholic is in his most natural element when he's at the head of a table moderating an important meeting, on set directing a movie scene-by-scene, or behind a podium delivering a rousing speech to an audience. The Workaholic filters thoughts through the rational side of his mind, so his emotions often lose to logic. He can be pragmatic to the point of suppressing his sentiments or abandoning them altogether in favor of efficiency. This leads to a loss of playfulness and lightheartedness. The Workaholic takes his duties so seriously that he can treat his home life like a job; in his mind he creates strict schedules even for his loved ones. He allots himself certain dates and times for playing with the kids, watching TV, even being intimate with his wife! He's so disciplined that there's not much room for spontaneity with the Workaholic, and play becomes disproportionate to work. When he's away from his work for too long, the Workaholic starts to feel unproductive and experiences symptoms of withdrawal like crashes in energy and hints of depression.

In fact, the Workaholic may be putting in those long hours to cover more than just the bills; psychology researchers at the University of Bergen in Norway found a strong link between workaholism and ADHD, OCD, anxiety, and depression. Whether these psychiatric problems arise from extended work, or extended work is a means of coping with such preexisting conditions, is unknown. The Workaholic doesn't always work because he finds it intrinsically pleasing, but because he feels an inner compulsion to work; his work may be his distraction from certain bothersome feelings or external pressures, or it may validate his worth to himself. In overworking himself, it's likely that the Workaholic is attempting to satisfy self-perceived shortcomings. Let's say that as a child, the Workaholic wasn't given enough liberty of thought or his parents rigidly controlled his behavior. He might grow up craving control and freedom of expression, settling on his work as a means of fulfillment and a way of dealing with things.

But working too much can have dire repercussions on health. According to the World Health Organization, burnout syndrome (BOS) is a work-related group of symptoms caused by heavy workload, long hours, diminished resources, and conflicts with coworkers, among other things. Chronic work-related stress will lead to energy depletion, a distant attitude toward one's work, and reduced personal accomplishment. When this happens, the Workaholic may ironically grow to despise his once-beloved work. Every Workaholic will experience occupational burnout sooner or later, and so may the average working person: in June 2019, *Forbes* magazine based an article on a recent Gallup study of nearly 7,500 full-time employees. Of them, nearly 23 percent reported feeling burned out at work very often or always, while an additional 44 percent reported feeling burned out sometimes.

Not all Workaholics are CEOs of big companies; your own Workaholic might be a nurse, accountant, or car salesman who simply puts in too many hours and too much effort. As every Workaholic will have to learn, too much of a good thing is never a good thing. He needs to keep his work addiction in check, or he risks losing more valuable aspects of life to it. The Workaholic can get his priorities mixed up, putting his ambitions before his children, his career before his health, and his money before his sanity. Life has a curious way of bringing us back toward the things that really matter, and sometimes a Workaholic has to suffer a rather brutal wake-up call to regain sight of what's most important. One of the Workaholic's primary goals, therefore, should be to reassess what brings him joy and admit the fact that it might not be work-related. This is a lesson not just for the Workaholic but for all of us: by all means, it is our right to have prosperity and abundance. We're allowed to have beautiful and expensive things, but we shouldn't allow them to have us. The Workaholic must enjoy what he works for in moderation, without allowing it to consume his heart or mind.

It's inevitable that his work will spill over onto his family. In psychology, displacement refers to an intense emotion that becomes internalized then transferred onto a new object. The new object is usually unrelated to the cause of the emotion. So if he had a bad day at work because a deal didn't go through, the Workaholic might come home and take it out on family members who didn't actually contribute to the problem. He might become distant, cold, irritable, or aggressive. When this happens, the Workaholic needs to be reminded that his work is affecting his loved ones and that it must be separated from his family life. Wait until the Workaholic isn't so focused on the predicament at work, then propose this to him gently. If you bring it up when he's still brooding over his work issue, the Workaholic might dismiss your argument and turn even moodier.

Sunita was married to a Workaholic named Raj who was the head of a big firm in New York City. Raj worked morning, noon, and night like a robot, but he loved what he did. For the first few years of their marriage, this wasn't such a problem, and the couple had two children. Sunita, a homemaker, was as sympathetic and patient as she could be. But as time went on, she started feeling more and more distant from Raj; all he seemed to care about was his work. Their children were growing up without a father, and his lack of presence was taking a toll on the whole family.

While Raj did bring home a lot of money, the expensive things Sunita could afford to buy didn't fill the space in her heart that grew bigger with each passing day. Sunita expected Raj to come home and spend some quality time with her, play with the kids, make plans for the future, and make love. Instead, she got a husband who barged into the house exhausted and desperate to sleep so he could wake up early again the next morning. He had no desire to talk about his day and rarely had enough energy to be intimate with Sunita. Raj didn't think he was doing anything wrong and, like a true Workaholic, believed Sunita couldn't appreciate the hard work that put Gucci bags in her closet and food on her table each day.

The situation continued in this manner for years without improvement. Eventually, Sunita reached her boiling point and gave up on being the "good housewife" who stayed home alone. She hired a nanny and started going out with her friends. Trying to compensate for the emptiness she felt, Sunita started drinking—a lot. Raj was noticing her absences, arriving home to find a nanny greeting him instead of his wife. He tried to talk sense into Sunita and convince her to stop going out, but she was rather enjoying her newfound freedom. She even found a lover (that Raj found out about), which added more strain to their relationship. Raj still wasn't comprehending that all it would take to rectify the situation was to give up a fraction of his career and give more attention to his family. To this day, Raj and Sunita find themselves in the same entanglement: a Workaholic who won't compromise and a fed up housewife who took matters into her own hands.

Not all Workaholics have problems with their families due to their workloads. Some are great at juggling work, home, and everything in between. Jonathan, a representative for an international software company, was strictly disciplined with his work. He traveled often to meet with potential clients but took his wife and kids with him whenever he could and spent time with them between meetings, which made up for his many trips. It still wasn't easy for his family and arguments did occur, but Jonathan's willingness to compromise kept everyone content. If the Workaholic can find that sweet balance between commitment to his career and commitment to his home life, he and his partner can enjoy great synergy.

Misconceptions about the Workaholic: Women interpret the Workaholic in one of two ways: they either accept his devotion to his work or they don't get it. The woman who can't come to terms with the Workaholic's full schedule feels ignored and rejected by him. She can't appreciate his loyalty to his job and takes personally the time he spends away from her. The woman who understands the value of a Workaholic's career has a much easier time coping with his frequent absences.

How he really thinks: Most Workaholics genuinely enjoy providing for those they love and see to it that their family members are well cared for, accomplishing almost superhuman feats to give them all they need. The justification for his excessive work is his ability to bring good with it to those he loves. However, this doesn't hold true for every member of this archetype.

Because the Workaholic has learned the value of a hard-earned dollar, he might become parsimonious, even with his own partner. You'd be surprised to know that some very wealthy men are quite frugal with their own wives. We've met plenty of women who boasted about having rich and powerful husbands, yet those same husbands kept them on strict allowances every week. This is another part of his personality that the Workaholic must work on: maintaining a healthy, measured relationship with money so that he doesn't become possessed by avarice or megalomania.

The Workaholic will regard a woman who can't accept his work as narrow-minded or, if she's benefiting materially from his efforts, downright ungrateful. He's turned on by a woman who's intelligent and business oriented like him. More than anything else, he appreciates the partner who approves of his work and supports him in striving for even more.

Can he commit? The Workaholic can offer not only commitment but financial stability as well. The catch is that he must be doing well in his career. When the Workaholic is unstable in his work, his partner will feel the effects.

Making a Workaholic commit entails that you embrace his career wholeheartedly. He may work long hours or have a hectic schedule, but once he's attached to you, you will become an indispensable part of his life. Have patience with the Workaholic when his job requires time, but also know when to ask for his time. Because the Workaholic has a habit of getting carried away with how much he works, there will be moments when you'll have to remind him to slow down and come home. Show the Workaholic that you respect his work and admire his talents. Helping him in little ways will go a long way: create a schedule for his deadlines, pack his lunch on ultra-busy days, confirm his appointments, and so on. Ask him about his day and offer advice when he needs it. He will appreciate your kind intentions and become more devoted to you. Though the

Workaholic is more rational than romantic, he still needs an outlet to release emotions that become bottled up due to the demands of his career. Encourage him to talk, relax, and engage in activities that discharge stress.

What he needs from you: The Workaholic's ideal relationship consists of teamwork and collaboration. He needs you to respect his work and, if possible, even help him at it. He wants you to push him to finish a project and motivate him before a meeting. The Workaholic would like you to handle your own problems and not be on top of him for every little thing. He asks that you understand how much he apprizes his career and that you be mindful of his professional time. In turn, he'll make time for you. The Workaholic gets along superbly with a businesswoman who is also dutiful at home.

We all like punctuality, but no one appreciates it more than the Workaholic, whose time equals literal money. Be on time for your dates with the Workaholic and look as sharp as if you were going to an interview! Delve into a few topics about his career during your time together.

Compatibility with the Workaholic: The Workaholic is most compatible with the Workaholic and the Independent. Two Workaholics work well because they'll keep busy in their own separate worlds but still be able to come home to a partner who loves them. Neither the Independent nor the Workaholic will bother or smother each other, which can also work out.

The Workaholic is least compatible with the Wounded Warrior and the Narcissist. The Workaholic doesn't have the time or patience to help the Wounded Warrior heal, and he certainly won't entertain the Narcissist's pretentiousness.

Differences between male and female Workaholics: The differences in which men and women express this archetype can be noted in their diligence to their family, particularly their children. Women are the more nurturing, caring gender by nature. Their maternal instincts will kick in even with the weight of work on their shoulders, and they'll still tend to the needs of their family first. The male Workaholic, on the other hand, relies on his woman to perform most of the housework. He may love his family dearly, but he most likely won't stop typing away on his laptop if he hears the little one crying from the other room. His reassurance comes from providing financially for his family; many Workaholic men believe this makes up for their lack of time or involvement at home.

Identifying qualities: Responsible, dependable, accomplished, goal-oriented, headstrong, motivated, independent, provider, overachiever, intelligent, fast-paced, great interpersonal skills, persuasive, values time, and self-made ethos.

Represented by: The lion. Like the lion, the Workaholic is the king of his jungle. He goes above and beyond to provide for his pack but needs a lioness to stand tall and strong by his side.

Real-life Workaholics: J-Lo, Beyoncé, and Jeff Bezos.

THE NARCISSIST

The Narcissist grapples with his ego, which
threatens to overtake his personality.
—Carmen Harra

The word *Narcissist* sprang from the Greek myth of Narcissus, a proud youth known for his striking beauty. One day, Narcissus was hunting in the woods when he saw his reflection in a lake and fell madly in love. He gazed at himself for so long that he was driven to madness and turned into a flower. True to legend, we've met some Narcissists who would gladly spend the remainder of their lives staring at their own splendid reflections.

The Narcissist has crossed the boundary from empowerment to entitlement. Where there is little humility and a lot of self-indulgence, one has entered the realm of privilege. It's not that the Narcissist is cold-hearted, but some Narcissists are more in love with themselves than they are with their partners.

The ego serves a critical role in protecting us from harm. When we act on our ego, we act in our favor and make decisions that benefit us. But when our ego gets carried away, it makes us do things that appear selfish, uncaring, and disrespectful. We start to think *only* about ourselves and little or not at all about others. The Narcissist's ego overpowers the more altruistic aspects of his personality. Ironically, narcissism often emerges from an inferiority complex: the Narcissist is afraid of not being as good as, as rich as, as good-looking as, or as powerful as other men. To alleviate these intimidations, he puts extra effort into proving he's the best. The Narcissist cares what other people think—*a lot.*

It's important to understand that most people who fit into this archetype don't actually suffer from narcissist personality disorder or NPD. We all display narcissistic bias from time to time, but that doesn't mean we have a personality disorder. NPD is rare according to the *Diagnostic and Statistical Manual of Mental Disorders*, with only 0.5 to 1 percent of the general population having this disorder. A person with NPD is next to impossible to date, so our archetypal version of the Narcissist is simply an individual whose ego has become hyperactive but is still manageable.

Narcissism can manifest on a broad spectrum, so a person can show a few self-centered hints here and there (like refusing to compromise with his partner once in a while) or have an increased need for attention and control. How narcissistic someone becomes varies as he passes through experiences that tame or amplify his ego. When archetypal narcissism does get out of hand and a person develops NPD (or other mental disorders), he may exhibit delusions of grandeur. These delusions are false beliefs that contradict reality and generally involve the Narcissist's greatness; he may believe he possesses a secret skill or talent, is famous, or was chosen for some special task. Someone with full-blown clinical NPD is convinced the entire galaxy revolves around him. If you believe you're dating a Narcissist, be on the lookout for such warning signs. And if you do spot them, urge the Narcissist to seek help.

Most Narcissists demonstrate a robust personality. They're extroverted, highly opinionated, the general life of the party, and drawn to adventure and the finer things in life. They enjoy female company and boasting about their possessions, success, and status, but they don't like their views or attitudes to be challenged. The Narcissist advertises himself wherever he goes, which can be exhausting to his other half. At some point, she'll roll her eyes and think to herself, "Yes, John, we get it, you're the best." Someone with a high severity of narcissism can come across as a big braggadocio, being both haughty and proud.

There exist two kinds of Narcissists: grandiose and vulnerable. Grandiose Narcissists need to show off to the world and usually assume assertive roles in society. One example of a grandiose Narcissist was Nicolae Ceausescu, the Romanian president who felt the need to build the biggest building in the country, called the Palace of the Parliament, for himself. Rumor has it that he created a structure of such proportions just so he could sleep in a different bedroom each day of the month (Ceausescu was assassinated before he got to live out this fantasy). It's interesting to note that Ceausescu was married to his spouse, Elena, for over forty years, until the day of their mutual deaths. Vulnerable, or covert, Narcissists present quite a different nature: they may come across as quiet or reserved. That's because they don't want to waste time dealing with inferior minds. To the vulnerable Narcissist, they're pretty close to perfect. But they also feel life has been unfair to them and, because of that, they often take on the role of a victim. Both types of Narcissists require that your focus is on them, so being in a relationship with a Narcissist can be emotionally consuming. There are Narcissists out there, both grandiose and vulnerable, who are undateable because their self-inflation has gone past the point of no return.

But if his selfishness is controlled, the Narcissist can keep up a good relationship. Ralph was a dear friend and an obvious grandiose Narcissist. Before going to a party, he needed to make sure he bought a brand-new outfit, buffed his nails, and washed his car until it was squeaky clean. He relished the attention and compliments he received. Nevertheless, Ralph maintained several long and relatively normal relationships; as much as he was obsessed with himself, he was also generous, loving, and kind to his partner. It also helped matters that he found pretty lenient girlfriends who accepted him for who he was. They let him flaunt what he had and encouraged him in his endeavors. Ralph was a Narcissist who go to the extreme; his tendencies were moderated.

Peter was a vulnerable Narcissist whose personality was initially difficult to detect. In his first session with us, he discussed his job and money—pretty typical subjects for male clients to bring up. But as time went on and he returned for more sessions, Peter began bringing up more "interesting" matters. He started confessing to how he used the people he worked with to his advantage. He pretended to befriend them and then, after he had gotten what he wanted, he cut them off abruptly. He divulged that he had been saving up his money and lied to his family about his financial standing when they asked him for help. Peter justified his actions this way: his father had passed away at the age of ten and Peter felt it was very unfair to him to have to grow up without a dad. Ever since then, he felt like the world was against him. Peter stated that he had been feeling like a victim all his life. If he didn't care about himself—and only himself—no one else would. "Not only would no one help me," he said during one session, "but everyone would hurt me." As we got to know him better, Peter's covert narcissism reared its ugly head. His egoistic outlook made it nearly impossible to maintain a healthy relationship with coworkers, family members, or a woman.

Misconceptions about the Narcissist: The Narcissist has a bad rep with women. And truth be told, he's *earned* the negative impression most women have when they think of a man who's selfish and pompous. Women believe a self-absorbed man can't possibly feel love for another human being. They expect the Narcissist to be mean and cold, when in reality most Narcissists are so warm and charming that their partners won't know they're self-centered until long into the relationship! The woman who does pick up on this early enough might back out of the relationship before the Narcissist has even had a chance to unveil his positive side to her.

How he really thinks: The Narcissist *does* want to improve himself. Deep down he sees his defects and wants to correct them, but his approach is flawed. So instead of admitting his faults and reflecting quietly on how he can mollify them, the Narcissist plays up his strengths and proclaims them to the world.

The irony is that in wanting to be the "best of the best," the Narcissist will try to please his partner in his unique and showy kind of style. This is the kind of man who needs to propose in front of an audience so that everyone applauds him. He wants to make sure that if the relationship ends, his partner will remember him as the best thing that ever happened to her. True to his character, he'll take the lead in his relationship and might even go out of his way to prove that he's a better man than any out there. The problem many times isn't the Narcissist's actions but the intentions behind his actions: he'll do the right thing not for the sake of doing something good but because it makes him look good. He'll compromise in the relationship, but it'll be in such a way that still benefits him. To the Narcissist, all things reflect back upon him.

It's not that the Narcissist is emotionally inept; he can develop deep and palpable feelings for his love interest. His partner must bear in mind that he is *not* the sociopath, who can't experience empathy. The issue is that too many of the Narcissist's feelings concern himself.

Can he commit? The Narcissist will commit to the woman who indulges him but who also indulges herself. Despite how much he's into himself, the Narcissist wants to see that his woman takes care of her needs too. The Narcissist likes to chase a woman because he loves proving that he can get what he wants, so his partner will have to play hard to get at times. Be careful not to insult the Narcissist or play on his weaknesses; his ego will shift into overdrive. He will overreact and put you down, after which he'll feel sorry for what he said and did. Express yourself gently to the Narcissist in regard to how he needs to improve or the things he needs to fix about himself. Reassure him of his strengths and the things he's done right first.

Just because a man is into himself doesn't mean he's can't extend love and devotion. The Narcissist can love you wildly and show you a good deal of affection. If the Narcissist sees that you accept his overzealous self-regard and even add a nice word here and there to boost his esteem, he will like you more and more. Constantly telling the Narcissist that he's a Narcissist will do nothing to lessen how fond he is of himself. It may even cause him to insult you, as the Narcissist retaliates harshly to criticism (even if it's meant to be constructive). But tending your own needs and desires, so that you equal his confidence level, will make the Narcissist see he's found the perfect self-loving match.

The Narcissist will do almost anything to get a reaction out of you because he likes to test just how emotionally involved you are with him. This is yet another consequence of his ego: the more you succumb to him emotionally, the more it strokes his ego. Writing entire novels to him that encompass your every feeling via text is not the way to win an argument with this archetype. If you do that, you only gift his ego with more of the emotional power you should be retaining for yourself. If you're having a disagreement with the Narcissist, it's wiser to respond to him with very few words because this will give him the impression that you don't care and that he needs to try harder (not to mention that it'll drive him crazy). Remember that the ego may be loud and proud, but it is also very fearful.

Perhaps the greatest drawback of being in a relationship with a Narcissist is that you'll feel he can't always reciprocate your intentions, emotions, and efforts fully. Especially if your nature is sacrificial, you will notice (sometimes painfully) that the Narcissist doesn't always return what you give; he doesn't give you little gifts like you give him and he won't think to pick up your favorite food on his way home. When this bothers you, you will need to speak up to the Narcissist and make him aware of his actions as well as what you would like him to do. Don't feel hurt or assume it's because he doesn't care. Each relationship type has copious flaws, but the Narcissist is especially complex. Some Narcissists can learn to reciprocate in a relationship and some will always fall short of giving their partner what she deserves. This depends on the degree of egoism present in your partner's personality.

What he needs from you: As you can guess, the Narcissist needs you to give him attention—lots of it. You'll have to be okay with the Narcissist stealing the spotlight often. You might even find the Narcissist becoming jealous of you! And we don't mean the typical kind of jealousy a man feels when his date is flirting with the waiter at dinner; we mean actual envy of you doing better than him. You may feel like you're in some weird sort of competition with the Narcissist, who strives to be the best out of all the people around him. Chivalry will be tossed out the window in a competition against the Narcissist: he won't let you win the tennis match just because you're a woman, or his partner at that. Let the Narcissist think he's wining, not because he's better than you in any way but because you see through his infatuation with himself and are smart enough not to take his personality flaws so seriously.

It's pivotal to the relationship to let the Narcissist win, but only up to a certain point. Once his complacency starts getting in your way or holding you back, it's time to address the issue. Now, bringing up issues to a Narcissist can be tricky because his ego will usually prevent him from seeing that he's doing anything wrong. He may get extremely defensive, since confrontation unseats the Narcissist from his cozy throne. There are a few approaches you can take to bring up a delicate issue with the Narcissist, perhaps the most effective of which is to use examples of similar cases. Do you have any mutual friends who have gone through experiences comparable to yours? If so, using their examples can open the Narcissist's eyes a bit. Ultimately, the most useful strategy is to explain to the Narcissist how your suggested changes or solutions will benefit him.

The woman who chooses to be with a Narcissist cannot be a weak woman; you can't doubt yourself or lack confidence. You'll have to be as tough as the Narcissist is to keep up a relationship with him.

Compatibility with the Narcissist: The Narcissist is most compatible with his own kind and with the Hopeless Romantic. Two Narcissists can feed off of each other's egos, especially if one is grandiose and the other is vulnerable. Take Kim Kardashian and Kanye West as an example. Kanye is a Narcissist in equal measure but he doesn't mind stepping aside and letting the cameras focus on Kim. The Narcissist will love the Hopeless Romantic's support and sacrifice but may also take advantage if his self-obsession isn't under control.

The Narcissist is least compatible with the Independent and the Workaholic. The Narcissist won't think it's worth it to put so much effort into making the Independent commit, and he won't appreciate the fact that the Workaholic can't spoil him with unlimited time and affection.

Differences between male and female Narcissists: More men are grandiose Narcissists. More women are vulnerable or covert Narcissists, making it easier for a woman to disguise narcissistic features. Narcissistic men like to show off; it validates their worth. Narcissistic women like to get everything they want, but don't always need to flaunt it to the world. As an example, Donald Trump, a clear Narcissist, needs to be vociferous and ostentatious. He savors being the center of attention. His wife, Melania, another clear Narcissist, is happy getting what she wants while patiently waiting behind the curtain. She comes across as a vulnerable Narcissist, judging by statements she's made about being bullied and treated unfairly. Male or female, grandiose or covert, the Narcissist's primary preoccupation is himself.

Identifying qualities: Self-absorbed, covetous, self-pampering, paranoid, a risk-taker, needs reassurance, rejects criticism, spontaneous, adventurous, jealous, charming, competitive, into his looks, proud, and needs to have his way.

Represented by: The king. Like the king, the Narcissist holds himself in royal regards. He wants to remain at the height of his power and prove his greatness to all who look up to him, including his queen.

Real-life Narcissists: Vladimir Putin, Madonna, and Mariah Carey.

THE FREE SPIRIT

The Free Spirit needs to decide who he is
before he can give a woman what she needs.
—Carmen Harra

We've all heard a popular song by Nelly Furtado that says,

> I'm like a bird
> I'll only fly away
> I don't know where my soul is
> I don't know where my home is.

Cue the Free Spirit. If this archetype had an anthem, "I'm Like a Bird" would be it. Most men in this group fly away from relationships and haven't been able to make themselves at home with a woman (at least not for long).

If you look him up in the dictionary, you'll read that a Free Spirit is "a person with a highly individual or unique attitude, lifestyle, or imagination." If you encounter him in real life, you'll see that this definition holds true: the Free Spirit is an outlier, a nonconformist. He enjoys going against trends and marching to the beat of a different drum.

This archetype is undecided in all that he does: from relationships to work to personal goals, the Free Spirit likely has trouble committing in multiple aspects of his life. He simply doesn't know what he wants. He may have a faint inkling, but when talking comes to doing, the Free Spirit usually can't execute. This man may claim he wants to have a relationship but abandons ship when things get serious. This can leave his partner bemused and blaming herself when, in reality, the Free Spirit's problem is not the woman but the notion of commitment itself. Unlike the Independent, who's afraid of losing his identity to his partner, the Free Spirit doesn't act on fear. All things considered, he's pretty courageous and bold! He finds it hard to stay still, both literally and figuratively, and likes to experiment with different things without getting attached to one. He experiences attachment issues on a subconscious level. Thus, the Free Spirit comes across as curiously detached from material possessions, religion, and even his family members. Some might call him a hippie.

The reason he doesn't settle on anything is because the Free Spirit hasn't discovered his sense of self. This was most likely caused by something out of his control as he was growing up. As a child, the Free Spirit may have been heavily influenced by his family or peers, never being allowed to think for himself. Or he may have lacked the parental stability needed to mold him into a stable adult. His mom and dad may have split then gotten back together. He may have had to move around a lot, maybe because his parents switched jobs or their careers demanded it. He may have changed schools several times, unable to maintain close friendships with other kids his age. The Free Spirit may have assumed multiple roles within the spectrum of high school personas. He could have been a jock one year then a goth the next. You're likely to find the cause of the Free Spirit's indecisiveness by inspecting the earlier part of his life, during which most of the human character is formed. If he's been like this from early on, then his whole life has been one phase after another; he floated along as time passed but never rooted himself into a firm identity.

If it's something that happened in his adult life, the Free Spirit might've undergone a huge shift that threw his entire existence into question. Maybe someone he was really close to passed away, or maybe he suffered a health problem or crisis that caused him to reevaluate who he really is and what he stands for, though he never received a clear answer. Even in his thirties, forties, or beyond, the Free Spirit hasn't yet painted a clear portrait of himself. As you can imagine, this erects a significant hurdle in his love relationships.

Stability is a challenge for the Free Spirit; he is impulsive, acting on the emotions he feels at the time. In the heat of the moment, the Free Spirit might tell you he loves you, but when he leaves your house, the love he just professed leaves as well. It's not that the Free Spirit wants to hurt women; this is just how he is. His entire personality isn't one at all because he never settled into his true self. He hasn't organized his thoughts and emotions enough to follow through on one way of thinking and doing. The moment he gets too comfortable anywhere, the Free Spirit uproots himself for reasons known only to him. Different personalities stream through this archetype, and he can transform with the seasons. This is an extraordinary character defect, because how, after so many years of living in disarray, does one get centered?

Because he's so easily influenced by external forces, the Free Spirit is neither here nor there. His friends hold great sway with the Free Spirit, who tends to go with the flow of things. He listens to others to the point of being emotionally corruptible. So if his buddies aid and abet him to party every night, that's bad. But if his partner encourages him to become better each day, that's good.

Of the seven archetypes, the Free Spirit is most likely to ghost you after the date you thought went so well; he seems to have invented the idea of mixed signals. He is transient in his emotions and elusive in his nature, flitting between wanting a woman and wanting to wander. His presence can be ephemeral, coming on strongly then disappearing for several days straight, and he can have mood swings, turning into a seemingly different person overnight. He also says one thing then does another, making promises he sometimes can't keep. He might promise you that you're going away on vacation next week, but next week, he might not remember to call. Once he sees the effort that's going to be required of him, he withdraws from the relationship. Certain things can trigger a switch in the Free Spirit and shift his intentions, like having a bad argument. If it's bad enough, it'll make him revisit everything he believes then pack his things and leave. The Free Spirit is the guy who breaks up with you by saying, "It's not you, it's me." Trust us, it's true—it really is him.

Some Free Spirits might even have a touch of borderline personality disorder, a mental illness characterized by a series of unstable relationships and a distorted sense of self. We all have a little "voice" inside our head that tells us what to do. Normally this voice is (or should be) guided by deep-seated beliefs of right over wrong. When you meet a new person you like, your voice tells you that you should be transparent with him. So you do things the "right" way by reply to his messages, telling the truth about yourself, showing up for the date, and so on. This is how it's supposed to work, but this is not the case for everyone. The Free Spirit can experience contradictory beliefs within himself. One voice might be telling him to get into a relationship while another might advise him to stay single. Not knowing which voice to trust, the Free Spirit tries to follow both. It's almost as if he has multiple personalities: he wants to settle down yet shakes off getting into a relationship; he's dependent on a woman yet wants to do things on his own. Though he sees the value in it, it can be truly difficult for the Free Spirit to commit.

The real problem is when the Free Spirit stays on the outside of society for too long. If he's a lifelong Free Spirit, he's the type of guy you see at a party, maybe in his fifties, who looks out of place and way too old to be there. We've all seen one or known one; he's either never gotten married or has gotten divorced six times. This is a serial dater who most likely went through several romances that crashed and burned before you met him. The Free Spirit can have bona fide feelings for a woman, but he doesn't know how to hold on to them for long enough. He therefore loses the momentum needed to build on his intentions. He bounces around, losing interest and going from conviction to confusion quickly.

Lucky for him, the Free Spirit emanates effortless swag and animal magnetism. His hair that's just a bit untidy, his eyes that seem to penetrate your soul—this type of man could charm the pants off of anyone, quite literally. Free-spirited men can be seen as "bad boys," since jumping from relationship to relationship and having a squeaky-clean reputation don't exactly go hand in hand. He can be an emotional nomad, roving around in his feelings without settling on one. This archetype is able to juggle multiple relationships at once without letting any get too far. Whereas other men can have two girlfriends and become seriously involved with both, the Free Spirit doesn't become emotionally intimate with any of his love interests. You can imagine how frustrating this is to the woman who genuinely likes a Free Spirit. She'll try to get close to the man she likes, only to have her efforts end in vain.

Amelia fell in love with Joshua twenty years ago. Even then, Joshua showed some signs of being a Free Spirit. Twenty years later, Amelia finds herself in the same place with her boyfriend, having made no emotional progress. Joshua claims that he likes Amelia, but he frequently moves around the country as his job demands, so he doesn't get to see her often. He's been stringing Amelia along with false promises, but he also casually dates other women, committing fully to no one. Joshua has never been married and has little desire to start a family. Despite our advice telling her otherwise, Amelia continues to pursue Joshua.

Some men in this archetype are notorious risk-takers—they love adventure and performing dangerous feats! And there may be a scientific explanation for this: the DRD4 gene is a dopamine receptor that regulates levels of dopamine in the brain. But a variant of this gene, called DRD4-7R and dubbed the "wanderlust gene," is less sensitive to dopamine. Studies show that about 20 percent of the population carry this variant gene, which means these individuals require greater stimulation to feel satisfied or rewarded. No one gene is responsible for a person's actions, but those carrying the wanderlust gene have more of a penchant to travel, experiment, and explore. They don't deal well with a routine or being tied down.

Fiona was dating a man named Brandon who had a habit of seeking thrills. It seemed that every time Fiona called Brandon to say hello, Brandon was too busy to talk. Once Brandon asked Fiona if he could call her back because he was about to bungee jump off a cliff, and another time he claimed he had to put his phone away because he was pulling on his scuba diving suit. This may be a comical (and true) example, but it highlights the libertine personality that many Free Spirits, especially those with the wanderlust gene, share in common.

There is a great deal of duality within the Free Spirit, who sees the pros and cons of anything. He views life through a broader perspective, almost like an outsider. Through the Free Spirit's mind pass all possibilities with equal conviction. The Free Spirit recognizes potential in everything he does, so he does see the potential of being in a relationship with the woman he likes, but he can't take the right actions and falls short. Though he doesn't act on fear of commitment, he feels a torrent of emotions that can be overwhelming. He wants to accomplish everything at once but ends up accomplishing very little or nothing. He's not necessarily scarred on the inside like the Wounded Warrior, nor does he esteem love to be greater than life like the Hopeless Romantic. He also doesn't regard himself too highly like the Narcissist. The problem, again, is that the Free Spirit hasn't built a strong foundation of self.

This can seem like a daunting archetype to work with, and many women simply don't have the time and patience to devote to a man who only commits halfway. But there is hope for the Free Spirit, as there is for anyone who wants to change. There have been many successful cases of Free Spirits settling down with one woman. Think of George Clooney, who fluttered from relationship to relationship for nearly thirty years before marrying human rights attorney Amal Almuddin in 2014.

Misconceptions about the Free Spirit: Many women quickly get fed up with the Free Spirit. They misread the Free Spirit's personality and label him as a womanizer. They often don't see beneath the playboy exterior and assume he's only out to hurt them. The Free Spirit doesn't want to hurt anyone, but his instinct may be telling him one thing, his brain another. In all actuality, by being so unsettled, he only ends up hurting himself: he sabotages his own chances of success, happiness, and progress by not being able to stay on track.

How he really thinks: It's not that he's a coward. Quite the contrary, the Free Spirit isn't afraid of committing to a relationship, but he might suddenly be struck by a different desire. He changes course halfway, whether it's on the day he plans to propose or the day he's about to tell his boss he's quitting. It's also not that he's stubborn, resistant to change, or attached to his freedom like the Independent. The Independent absolutely knows he wants to be Independent; he has decided that's what's best for him (until the right woman shows him otherwise). The Free Spirit simply isn't sure. He's just as tempted by the idea of a stable relationship as he is by being single and having fun. He is capable of mutability and evolution, but he needs that extra shove in climbing the next step of the ladder. The Free Spirit can't choose between one or the other, so he just wants everything. He conveniently fails to recognize that life doesn't work that way.

If the Free Spirit does fear anything, it's failure. He doesn't like to undertake the effort to achieve something, whether it's a long-term relationship or successful career, because it might not work out. His underdeveloped sense of self becomes evident here: goals seem intimidating to him because he doesn't believe enough in himself. In contrast to the Well-Rounded One, he handles responsibilities poorly and prefers to run away instead of resolving things. But the Free Spirit doesn't want to remain undecided all his life; he craves stability like any other sane person.

Can he commit? Putting intention into action is where the Free Spirit gets stuck. He can only give you something solid once he's solid in himself; he must first discover what he stands for. The Free Spirit needs to build a strong sense of self, underline his life values, and set up attainable goals. He must learn how to commit seriously to something before he can commit to a love relationship. Stability is vital to the Free Spirit, the kind of stability a loving and patient partner can help to instill.

What he needs from you: The first thing you should do for the Free Spirit you love is help him condense his sundry of thoughts and emotions. You will have to show him how to manage conflictual tendencies so that he learns how to allow his emotions to come and go without always acting on them. Feeling frustrated with his job from time to time, for instance, is not enough reason to actually leave his job (especially if he doesn't have a backup). Set little goals for him and assist him in completing them. Encourage him to carve one path for himself and stay on it. Remind him how rewarding it is to commit to something and see it through to the end. The more he learns how to stick to one job, project, or belief, the more likely the Free Spirit is to stick to one relationship.

To teach him how to pull through on his personal commitments, you'll have to help the Free Spirit home in on his authentic self and act on it. Anchor the Free Spirit in one area of his life, then another, then another. Then, once he's grounded in purpose, the Free Spirit can finally commit. This archetype reminds us why attaining self-knowledge is so important in knowing who we are, what we want, and what we can deliver to another person. Only a woman with a well-established identity can help a Free Spirit set up his own self. She will be instrumental in his life.

Compatibility with the Free Spirit: It's tricky to place the Free Spirit on a scale of compatibility and decide with which archetype he fits best because indecisiveness can ruin a relationship with even the most complaisant partner. At the end of the day, the Free Spirit is most compatible with the Hopeless Romantic, who believes in him enough to guide the Free Spirit to find himself.

The Free Spirit has little future with an Independent, as both partners will live in separate worlds and quickly go their separate ways. His fickle nature also won't inspire an Introvert to open up or a Wounded Warrior to heal.

Differences between male and female Free Spirits: There are as many women in this category as there are men. We've all heard of the runaway bride who suddenly gets cold feet before walking down the aisle and sprints away in her wedding gown. Women in the modern world are becoming more hesitant to commit for various reasons. But in general, it's still easier for free-spirited women to settle down in a relationship than it is for free-spirited men.

Identifying qualities: Capricious, unreliable, withdraws suddenly, makes big plans, reneges on his promises, unsure of himself, can't stay in one place, goes through phases, prone to identity crises, easily influenced, weak sense of self, and impulsive.

Represented by: the nomad. Like the nomad, the Free Spirit wanders without settling down. Constantly drifting along the outskirts, the Free Spirit takes the less beaten path by not conforming to the dictates of society.

Real-life Free Spirits: Gerard Butler, Hugh Hefner, and Tom Cruise.

Chapter 7

THE "WE" ARCHETYPES:
THE HOPELESS ROMANTIC,
THE WOUNDED WARRIOR,
AND THE INTROVERT

THE HOPELESS ROMANTIC

*To the Hopeless Romantic, life
is love and love is life.*
—Carmen Harra

In literature, Hopeless Romantics are characters who value love more than life itself. They're usually protagonists who sacrifice their own lives to save the one they love from mortal peril.

The real-world Hopeless Romantic is not much different: he bursts into a relationship like a medieval knight charges into battle, ready to risk it all for the maiden's hand in marriage. He is on a constant, quixotic quest to secure a life partner. He believes love is the only reward one can call his own.

The Hopeless Romantic is the kind of guy who proposes one month after he meets you. He wholeheartedly believes in love, which is admirable, but this can also make him aimless and tactless. You might be thinking, "Well, that's okay, he's just ready for commitment," but in all actuality it's not okay: the Hopeless Romantic is blemished by exaggerated love. He may throw himself into relationships blindly or fall in love with the wrong women altogether.

If you're on the receiving end of a relationship with a Hopeless Romantic, you might feel overwhelmed. He'll come on strongly and be needy of your time and attention. If you don't reciprocate these things, The Hopeless Romantic will get offended and think there's something wrong with him. Rather than take a step back, he'll come on even more strongly. He might try to control your life, thinking he's doing you a favor or showing you the right way. The Hopeless Romantic has a propensity for self-destruction (albeit lower than that of the Wounded Warrior), especially when he's hurting in love. There's no coping with a breakup the normal way for him; he must do something extreme to help him forget, like drinking or sleeping around or moving to a different state!

Being a Hopeless Romantic alters the way you view relationships, according to a study published by the *Journal of Social and Personal Relationships*. A Hopeless Romantic might be setting himself up for failure by having unrealistic expectations in a relationship, but he also has a more positive opinion of his partner overall; he might make excuses for his girlfriend or make himself believe that she's meeting his expectations when in reality she's not. Those who held romantic beliefs about their relationship were also more satisfied in their relationship, says the study. In other words, Hopeless Romantics aren't easily discouraged and tend to see the good in their partners, whether that good exists or not. The Hopeless Romantic is a people pleaser, or rather, a partner pleaser. He is inherently noble and altruistic and he thrives when he's doing good for others, especially the person he loves most.

Jayden was a classic Hopeless Romantic. He was in love with a woman named Gia, but Gia was complicated, to say the least. Gia, a Wounded Woman, had been traumatized in her former relationships and carried emotional scars with her. Jayden was incredibly patient with Gia. There were times when she had emotional outbursts and cried over little things. Most of the other archetypes would've run away from Gia, but Jayden firmly believed he could help her achieve emotional stability through patience, kindness, and caring. Little by little, he helped Gia see that he wasn't going to hurt her and she could trust him.

Gia's wounds of many years began to heal within months. Jayden did many things for Gia and expressed his desire to be with her no matter what, but he was more of a practical Hopeless Romantic: Jayden acknowledged that it would be a long time before Gia regained complete emotional health, and he was prepared to embark on this journey. He also knew that he couldn't take things too fast with Gia—he couldn't move in with her or settle down with her—until she was whole again. Out of love for her, Jayden was okay with making these sacrifices. In this case, the couple had a happy ending and are continuing to make progress together.

By contrast, Lorraine was in a disastrous relationship with Scott, a malignant Narcissist who bordered on sociopathy. It didn't help matters that Lorraine was an extreme Hopeless Romantic who just wouldn't give up on the man she loved. Scott alternated between inviting Lorraine into his home, then kicking her out for any little thing she did that generated his rage. Lorraine, however, remained valiantly undeterred: she bought gifts for Scott, cleaned his house, and even babysat his kids from a previous marriage! Like all Hopeless Romantics, Lorraine was convinced that the more good deeds she performed for her boyfriend, the more he would change. She truly believed her sacrifices could improve their dynamic so that she and Scott could be together long term. Sadly, their tumultuous relationship was in the same place two years later: Lorraine gave and Scott took. Lorraine was an example of a Hopeless Romantic who was completely illogical, out of touch with reality, and even self-destructive.

We recommended to Lorraine to exit this one-sided relationship and give herself the love that Scott obviously couldn't give to anybody but himself. But Lorraine's "love is larger than life" mentality wouldn't let her walk away. At the same time, she knew something was terribly wrong and didn't want to suffer anymore. So we applied a different strategy and suggested to Lorraine to go just one week without communicating with Scott—no picking up his calls or responding to his texts. Desperate to improve her situation, Lorraine accepted. She was disciplined and stayed away from him in every respect. At the end of that week, Lorraine called us and asked if it was okay to talk to Scott now; he had been blowing up her phone for seven days straight and even showed up in front of her house (she had locked the doors and turned off the lights). But we told her firmly, "No, go one more week. Just one more. Then, you can pick up."

That second week was perhaps the most difficult of Lorraine's life. She was resisting something that went against the nature of a Hopeless Romantic, pushing away a man she so desperately loved. Yet something was transforming inside Lorraine: her need to speak to or see Scott was receding. She was focusing on herself after a long time and doing what she wanted each day, which felt amazing. After that week passed, Lorraine called us again. We told her that if she really wanted to, she could call Scott back now, to which she responded, "No, I think I'll wait another week…or longer." That was the best thing we could've heard her say. If a Hopeless Romantic is able to step back and view his relationship in realistic terms, he can make sound decisions.

Misconceptions about the Hopeless Romantic: Most women feel that the Hopeless Romantic imposes on their lives too much. This is why the Hopeless Romantic often experiences problems in love; he scares his woman away! A Hopeless Romantic almost always comes on too strongly, and this is likely to turn off even the most well-rounded partner. His relative harmlessness and good intentions become evident in time, but he sometimes has to work extra hard to conquer his woman because of his intense manner.

How he really thinks: The Hopeless Romantic's tragic flaw is his recklessness in the name of love; he can become thoughtless just to please his partner. He might suddenly say, "Let's run away and get married!" but he hasn't yet thought about where you're running away to or how you'll pay the bills (to him these are just minor details, so long as he's with you).

The Hopeless Romantic can lose touch with reality if he's too set on reaching his ideal of love. He yearns for commitment but doesn't know how to approach it in a thoughtful, calculated way. He falls so head-over-heels in love that he won't realize if his partner is actually an awful person. He takes all that his other half says at face value, so you can imagine that it's not too hard to lie to a Hopeless Romantic who's in love with you. The definition of a daydreamer, the Hopeless Romantic remains blind to the truth by choice; this is the type of partner who, despite evidence, refuses to believe that the person he loves is cheating on or lying to him. He'll return again and again to identical scenarios, convinced that they'll end differently this time. We spoke earlier about cognitive dissonance, which is the state of having thoughts that are inconsistent with reality. This is when knowing and doing are polar opposites, and we willfully choose to do something that's harmful to us. The Hopeless Romantic is often guilty of cognitive dissonance, knowing his partner isn't good for him yet choosing to stay in the relationship. His notion of love is so great that he sees it as a panacea; he sincerely believes that if he loves hard enough, it will fix all his problems. Not so.

Can he commit? You already know the Hopeless Romantic is lofty, living with his head in the clouds. But far more important is the fact that his intentions are genuinely good: he just wants to give and receive love. He's been ready to commit since before he met you. This archetype is unlikely to cheat on you because he tends to become infatuated with one woman and one woman only. Unlike the Introvert, the Hopeless Romantic is completely open and wears his heart on his sleeve. To keep up a durable relationship with him, you'll have to ground the Hopeless Romantic in the real world and teach him how to exercise practicality and reasonable expectations. You'll have to take the reins with this type of guy; be firm with the Hopeless Romantic and set healthy boundaries without hurting him. Show him that it's okay to put himself first and you second and that you won't love him any less for it. Let the Hopeless Romantic do things for you because that brings him joy but stop him from going over the top or exhausting himself. Help him get organized in accomplishing goals for himself. If you can make him comprehend that a well-founded, slow-paced relationship is paramount, then you can go far with the Hopeless Romantic.

What he needs from you: The Hopeless Romantic needs you to teach him practicality without hurting his feelings. He does well with a partner who takes control in a healthy way and anchors him down. Show him that slow progress is true progress. The Hopeless Romantic is happiest when he's sacrificing for his loved one, so by all means let him bring a smile to your face, but make sure that you give him what he deserves too.

Compatibility with the Hopeless Romantic: The Hopeless Romantic is most compatible with the Wounded Warrior. It is in the nature of Hopeless Romantics to help, heal, and have compassion for their partners, which is what Wounded Warriors need to overcome their traumas. As long as he doesn't push too hard, a Hopeless Romantic can also fare well with an Introvert; his sincerity and enthusiasm will inspire an Introvert to open up.

The Hopeless Romantic is least compatible with the Independent, as the latter will quickly feel asphyxiated by the former. Although he'll love the attention he gets from a Hopeless Romantic, the Narcissist might exploit his good and giving heart. Two Hopeless Romantics will live in a la-la land together, feeding off of each other's imagination, which might not get them too far in the real world.

Differences between male and female Hopeless Romantics: The ways in which Hopeless Romantics engage in relationships can differ between the sexes. The Hopeless Romantic man will do his best to secure his woman by "tying her down," either through marriage, moving in together, or having a child. He'll try to win her over by showing her that he's everything she could ever dream of. The Hopeless Romantic woman will show unyielding sacrifice for the man she loves, going out of her way to tend to his every need. She might also pause her personal goals for him, like putting off having a family or starting a career. Both Hopeless Romantic genders love a challenge in love!

Identifying qualities: Loving, sentimental, sacrificial, impractical, needy, easily deluded, good-hearted, selfless, intense, lofty, steadfast, enthusiastic, impetuous, innocent, risk-taker, reckless, chivalrous, romantic, courageous, idealistic, and doesn't take no for an answer.

Represented by: The knight. Like the knight, the Hopeless Romantic charges into the battle of winning his lady's heart. He approaches a relationship the way a knight approaches a mission appointed to him, risking it all to prove his loyalty.

Real-life Hopeless Romantics: Princess Diana, Adele, and John Legend.

THE WOUNDED WARRIOR

The Wounded Warrior's past constantly intrudes in his present.

—Alexandra Harra

The Wounded Warrior deserves to be called a warrior because he's weathered some serious storms in life and emerged in one piece. Consequently, he knows two worlds: the world on the outside and the world on the inside, and they are as different as night and day. He oscillates between these two versions of reality, but the façade he puts on for the outside world doesn't match the turmoil he feels in his inside world. This archetype usually has an "escape," which can be anything from traveling to drugs to food to a talent. More often than not, this escape is adverse in nature. When the Wounded Warrior has had a few too many drinks (or is otherwise under the influence), he might slip and disclose events that happened to him long ago.

In truth, the Wounded Warrior is wracked with the pangs of his past. He may have abandonment issues because of a missing parent figure or a former lover who left him. The Wounded Warrior reminds us that the work that needs to be done first is within us. We're so keen to do our work on the outside—to make money, be successful, and buy objects—that we neglect what must be built, fixed, and secured inside.

Anthony Bourdain and Kate Spade both committed suicide in 2018. These two successful celebrities established empires in the material world but were hurting badly in their personal lives. Bourdain experimented with a number of drugs in his youth and divorced or separated twice. Spade combated depression and anxiety in silence. Both of these powerhouses seemed to be dealing perfectly well to outsiders, but inside themselves they were struggling. They didn't adequately address or know how to resolve inner problems, which led them to their last resort: taking their own lives.

In Jungian psychology, the shadow is the aspect of one's personality that's not acknowledged. It is comprised of character traits we don't like to examine or admit we have. It can be highly uncomfortable to explore our shadow side and face our failings and sometimes rough instincts. Despite this, the Wounded Warrior is buried in his shadow and immersed in self-perceived weaknesses. He feeds off its depths, where there is turmoil and conflict. This is why the Wounded Warrior tends to self-destruct as he is thrown further off balance. He can, with no warning, veer into immensely dark territory. One defining marker of the Wounded Warrior is going from a good to a bad mood within the blink of an eye because some unjustifiable trigger just hurled him back into the void. It can be something someone said, like a coworker taking a tiny jab at him, or something someone did, like his girlfriend forgetting to say she loves him before leaving the house. The Wounded Warrior personalizes everything, and for this reason, he is quick to put himself down when his flaws are being scrutinized. He might say, "I know he was better than me," or, "You loved him more than me, didn't you?" The feeling of not being enough or not being good enough rebounds every so often. He takes things personally or entirely the wrong way, assuming the role of a victim. This becomes frustrating for a Wounded Warrior's partner, who will feel like she has to walk on eggshells to prevent her sensitive significant other from relapsing into dangerous depths.

It's possible that some Wounded Warriors also suffer from post-traumatic stress disorder. We've met many people who have this disorder but either don't see the payoff of going to therapy or don't want to bother, so they continue to live with their emotional injuries and experience troublesome relationships as a result. Trauma suffered during the Wounded Warrior's younger years can become a lifelong psychological handicap, embedding itself into his identity. Unless he works to remove it, he will forever revert to it. The trauma may impede him from fully transitioning into his next phase of life.

Blessings may be waiting to materialize for the Wounded Warrior, but they can't do so until his wounds are mended. A Wounded Warrior is enmeshed in the emotions of an ordeal: guilt, regret, shame, resentment, etc. Often the Wounded Warrior feels guilty that he didn't do more to stop something bad from happening or to help someone he loved. This lingering sense of regret infects his other emotions; the moment a Wounded Warrior starts to feel happy, excited, or carefree, remorse reels him back into the shadow. The Wounded Warrior doesn't believe he's worthy of good; his thoughts circle back to "this can't actually be happening for me," so he blocks positivity from reaching him. The Wounded Warrior has to go back and heal the wound before he can heal himself.

One of our clients named Oliver lost his mother quite suddenly at a young age. He took to alcohol and cigarettes after her passing and couldn't quit because these habits had turned into addictions. Oliver was never able to heal from this event, and its effects seeped into his relationships; he got married and started a family, but the memory of his mother's death never left him. Oliver's wife showed him empathy and urged him to seek professional help, but the pain was too walled-up for Oliver to open up to her or anyone else. Whenever Oliver drank, he would bring up his mother with heartbreaking nostalgia. Oliver lost his own life to cancer that developed from smoking for so long. This real-life case demonstrates how difficult it can be to help a Wounded Warrior, who may or may not recover from disturbing experiences.

A Wounded Warrior can become downright cynical. He does this as a defense mechanism almost without thinking: to him, if you expect nothing or expect everything to go wrong, you're less likely to get hurt. So if his loved one disappointed him once, the Wounded Warrior will expect worse disappointments to come. It's important not to hurt him, as he'll dwell on your actions for a long time. Out of fear of being hurt again, the Wounded Warrior may hurt others. As you learned in chapter 3, people either perpetuate the things that were done to them or they do completely the opposite to others. How a person acts after a traumatic experience depends on whether he or she has been able to process emotions sufficiently. It can be especially difficult for a Wounded Woman to recover from sexual assault and subsequently be in a normal relationship.

Carla was raped in high school. This horrific experience left her with a subconscious imprint that she wasn't able to erase for nearly a decade. In her twenties, Carla got married to Rachel, and their relationship was anything but stable or healthy. Her wife was somewhat of a Hopeless Romantic who loved to sacrifice for Carla and tried everything to make her happy. Unfortunately, nothing seemed to work because Carla hadn't made peace with the memory of the incident from her past. Instead of appreciating her loving and dedicated partner, Carla abused Rachel verbally and emotionally. She collected all the pain that had been inflicted on her from the assault and unleashed it on her spouse.

Devoted though she was, Rachel was ready to give up on Carla. One day during an argument, Rachel blurted out, "I do everything for you but nothing's good enough. Don't you see how miserable you are, when you have no reason to be? You do it to yourself!" This struck a chord in Carla's mind: *What if Rachel's right? What if I am doing this to myself?* Carla started reflecting on her emotions from day to day and soon realized there was nothing really wrong with her life, only with her thinking: she had no real reason to get so upset over little things or be so insecure all the time. As she began recognizing the reality of her own self-destructive tendencies, Carla vowed to change.

She told Rachel that she wanted some time to herself and moved back into her parents' place. Carla spent time alone and meditated. She cried, a lot. She forced herself to recount what had happened in high school while reminding herself that the incident was long gone. She went to see a hypnotherapist to try and remove some of the negative impressions that had remained in her mind. She cried some more. She wrote down how she envisioned her life and what steps she could take to manifest it. Most of all, Carla started affirming to herself that good things *could* happen to her. And they did.

The Wounded Warrior needs to undergo this catharsis, this emotional purge, to help break up traces of trauma and release them from his being. It is through such effusions of grief that the Wounded Warrior is capable of incredible change. Like a phoenix bursting into flame and reborn from its ashes, the Wounded Warrior rises from his own sorrow no longer wounded but whole.

As the Wounded Warrior is mending, expect a radiant part of his personality to surface. Underneath the archetype of the Wounded Warrior is a vibrant and hopeful individual. If he's able to overcome his distress and resettle into normality, the Wounded Warrior makes a wonderful companion. He gathers his painful experiences and transmutes them into wisdom and enlightenment. As he reforms into the Well-Rounded One, he will be a joy to be around. And he will splendidly repay the partner who has remained by his side throughout the process with the gift of unconditional love.

Misconceptions about the Wounded Warrior: Women see the Wounded Warrior as troubled or complicated when in reality, he's simply hurt and doesn't know how to express that. His frustrations make him prone to emotional outbursts. A woman (like the intuitive being she is) will quickly pick up on the divergence that exists inside the Wounded Warrior. At the same time, it's all too easy to misinterpret him because his actions make him seem irresponsible, intolerable, and irrational. A woman might think her Wounded Warrior is just being dramatic, but the truth is that he doesn't know how to articulate his pain and is used to being misunderstood by those around him.

How he really thinks: People who have suffered damage tend to be insular, wanting to be detached from a group and by themselves. But being alone only intensifies the discomfort one feels inside. The Wounded Warrior has demons that he doesn't want to face and willfully suppresses. He doesn't know how to go about overcoming his pain, so he masks and buries it. The Wounded Warrior wants to be loved, but he's afraid of being hurt again. Instead of giving away his love, he hoards it up within himself. He needs someone to pry open his heart with great care.

You're likely to meet obstacles in doing so; the Wounded Warrior is resistant to change and notoriously stubborn. Think of adopting a dog that was abused in its previous home. That dog won't understand you only want to help and thinks you'll hurt him more, so he might growl and bite when you try to get close. A similar concept applies to the Wounded Warrior. He's hesitant to accept help, hence the need to make the Wounded Warrior trust you first by being gentle and compassionate.

Can he commit? When he's in his doldrums, the Wounded Warrior is emotionally cumbersome, becoming overly sensitive and pessimistic. If he remains within the frame of his archetype, the Wounded Warrior is limited in how far he can get in a relationship. The irony is that it's not because he can't commit but because of his own behavior: the dynamic with his partner will frequently turn tumultuous and unstable. If he confronts his inner demons and clears away traumatic imprints, the Wounded Warrior is perfectly capable of having a normal, loving connection.

The Wounded Warrior wants to fill his voids with love, but you must reassure him first. Remind him that he's not alone; everyone is fighting multiple battles on the inside at any given moment, including you! It matters not what he endured in the past because life sometimes puts us in situations for which we could never prepare. Assure the Wounded Warrior that there's no shame in having been hurt. What counts is that he came out stronger and wiser than before.

What he needs from you: If you want the Wounded Warrior to commit, you'll have to help him blend his inner and outer sides. You will have to gently and patiently unravel his pain, then show him how convert it into power. Many people try to get their answers from the outside. This is typical but completely ineffective; the outside world can't help you resolve what's damaged on the inside. The Wounded Warrior needs a woman to encourage him to reconcile his past and bridge the two elements of his being that make up one whole and courageous individual. Above all, the Wounded Warrior needs compassion from you. He will drive you crazy at times with his insecurities, but you'll have to remain focused on the greater scope of your actions: your relationship depends on his healing.

Compatibility with the Wounded Warrior: The Wounded Warrior is most compatible with the Hopeless Romantic. The Hopeless Romantic has sympathy for the Wounded Warrior and enough patience to take him by the hand through the healing process.

The Wounded Warrior is least compatible with his own archetype, the Narcissist, the Independent, and the Free Spirit. Two wounded partners won't motivate each other to make emotional progress. The Wounded Warrior will think the Narcissist is trying to hurt him and will misconstrue the Independent's lack of communication as something personal. The Free Spirit will promise the Wounded Warrior dedication but might leave him in the middle of the road, which is not an experience this already delicate archetype can afford to go through.

Differences between male and female Wounded Warriors: Both men and women can become emotionally fragile if they're wounded, but their coping mechanisms differ. Women may isolate themselves more often and develop depressive or anxious tendencies more easily. Men may externalize their emotions in detrimental ways like drinking or sleeping around so as not to have to deal with their feelings. Women are more open to feeling their pain, while men are more reluctant to succumb to it. This is possibly why the risk for depression and anxiety is higher in women. There's a notable decrease in self-care in both sexes. Some Wounded Warriors lose interest in upkeeping their appearance. On the other hand, men and women alike are capable of hiding their wounds so well that only those closest to them can detect something is wrong.

Identifying qualities: Distrustful, closed off, unsteady, indecisive, sensitive, insecure, pessimistic, has good intentions, fluctuates between extremes, experiences pain deeply, feels helpless, wants to escape, self-destructive, lives in the past, and has hidden talents.

Represented by: The soldier. Like the soldier, the Wounded Warrior has passed through some serious personal battles. He has suffered a fair share of losses and emotional injuries and must now find the resilience to heal.

Real-life Wounded Warriors: Michael Jackson, Eminem, and Judy Garland.

THE INTROVERT

*The Introvert is emotionally self-sufficient; he
recharges by spending time with himself.*
—Alexandra Harra

They say we live in an Extrovert's world. This is the case in United States, where 50 to 75 percent of Americans are Extroverts. Introverts and Extroverts are two major personality types in psychology. It's easy to recognize the Extrovert: sociable, agreeable, bold, and comfortable in the spotlight. Archetypes like the Independent, Workaholic, and Narcissist are noticeably extroverted. But how do you know when you're dating an Introvert? Some people think Introverts are the wall-flowers at a party, and they're partly right. The giveaway, however, won't be that he's shy or socially awkward or prefers staying in to going out (though he might). Many Introverts are excellent at cam-ouflaging themselves as Extroverts! The Introvert's markers are men-tal: the way he processes reality will reveal his true nature. And his unique way of being will show in his close connections. We chose to focus only on the Introvert as an archetype because Extroverts are less complex and therefore less of a challenge to date.

The Introvert is silently compelling. This is what may have drawn you to him in the first place: the innate sense of mystery that surrounds him, that quiet sort of language that speaks volumes. He didn't gain your attention through comedic exhibitions or a larger-than-life personality but through his meek magnetism. The Introvert is the kind of guy you meet in a bookstore browsing through some old volume or in the corner of a coffee shop on his laptop, but then he looks up and fixes you with a furtive gaze, and you instantly want to find out much, much more. The Introvert is understated but undoubtedly powerful. Think of an iceberg; you can only see its tip protruding the surface. You can't imagine that underneath the water is a monumental mass capable of sinking the *Titanic*.

What you soon discover is that the Introvert's biggest problem is his lack of communication. This can be misinterpreted by his part-ner as something done on purpose. The Introvert's gentle disposition developed during his childhood, and his reservations are not based on former experiences in love; they are subsumed into his personality. He contends with his hesitation to trust and his inability to express what he feels. There is a discrepancy between what's kept on the inside and what's shown on the outside, but not in a dangerously harmful way like the Wounded Warrior. While he doesn't normally self-destruct, the Introvert does need to uncage some of his inner being and introduce it to the outer world. He needs to realize that it's okay to share: his abundant emotions, his many brilliant ideas, and his fascinating theories about the world. The Introvert needs to be shown that he can have a tremendous impact on others if he simply opens up.

One of the reasons he might not want to is because the Introvert is very stable within himself. He can answer his own questions, form his own opinions, and follow his superb intuition without fail. Seldom does he seek guidance or fall into confusion. People open up to the Introvert effortlessly, but he rarely returns the energy. His art is listening, not talking. The Introvert already has everything he needs inside, so he'll only let in people who can contribute to his stability. He's like a steel fortress that very few can access; to enter, you must show that you come bearing good intentions.

Introverts take a longer time thinking things over and making important decisions than their extroverted counterparts. They feel the need to hold an entire mental debate before they can come up with a choice, weighing every side to the story. This makes them feel more confident in their decisions. Because Introverts are emotionally intelligent, they also take into consideration the way they feel. If you ask an Introvert for advice on making a decision, he'll probably remind you of what happened last time you made that decision. If the Free Spirit is impulsive, the Introvert is compulsive; when an unpleasant thought enters his mind, he will study it a thousand times from every angle until he can either reconcile it or make sense of it. Because of this, Introverts can turn obsessive. If you give the Introvert a task, expect that it might take him a bit longer than most people to complete but that he will execute it perfectly.

A person can turn inward after a painstaking ordeal. He or she may become a combination of the Wounded Warrior and Introvert. We knew a famous singer who performed regularly in front of tens of thousands of people. This lady kept up a stellar career for many years, until tragedy struck her personal life. She found out that her husband was cheating on her with a member of her band. To add insult to injury, he divorced her and left her with a small child. The woman retreated into her home and developed agoraphobia. She went from singing in front of large audiences every week to being afraid to step out of her house for groceries. The singer felt deep shame, embarrassment, and rejection. She was wounded but also turned completely introverted after this terrible experience.

On the whole, introversion is usually the result of nature, not nurture. Felicia liked a man named Jay. He was sweet, mild-mannered, and courteous. She suggested going out sometime and Jay agreed; he even told her to pick the time and place. Felicia found it odd that a man would step back and let the woman plan their first date, but she agreed nonetheless. There was a fair in town, and Felicia thought it would be cute to play games and get on some rides together. When they met outside the fair entrance, Felicia noticed that Jay's face fell. "What's wrong?" she asked. He worked up a smile and said, "Nothing, nothing's wrong."

As the evening wore on, it was clear that Felicia was enjoying herself, hauling around a giant stuffed bear and picking at her cotton candy, but Jay was not; he kept his hands in his pockets and glared at the screaming kids and rides whizzing by. By the time Felicia got home that night, she was convinced that Jay had had a horrible time and didn't like her at all.

But Jay called Felicia the next morning and thanked her for inviting him out. He kindly asked her to pick a "quieter" place next time. Felicia was again baffled as to why she had to do the planning, but she selected a cozy, romantic restaurant as the setting for their next date. When Jay showed up, he expressed to her that this was perfect. He confessed that he had felt a bit overwhelmed at the fair. Felicia couldn't fathom why, but she was still sympathetic to Jay. Little by little, Felicia came to know and appreciate Jay's introverted personality: he preferred staying in to going out, reading to watching TV, and discussing deep topics to pop culture. The more Felicia showed her good intentions, the more Jay's personality burgeoned before her eyes. Felicia inspired a sense of trust in Jay, which prompted him to bare his intricate self to her.

Misconceptions about the Introvert: Many women (and many people in general) aren't sure how to interpret the Introvert; he is shrouded in mystery. A woman might have a hard time discerning whether the Introvert is really into her or not. Since society has taught us that men should be in charge, some women deem the Introvert's meekness a deal breaker. Unless his partner is also an Introvert, the introverted man can be a challenge to decode; many women will become frustrated and impatient with the Introvert's caution and reticence. Although he appears nondescript on the outside, the Introvert houses a creative world within. He places emphasis on his inside before his outside, recognizing the value of having more than good looks or charm.

How he really thinks: The Introvert thinks it's better to keep things to himself, and this is not necessarily because he doesn't trust you; he thinks his partner won't understand his unique ideas or special ways of thinking, so he chooses not to share them. Too much external stimuli at once is unpleasant to the Introvert, as his senses are easily overloaded. So the Introvert is perfectly content with curling up with a good book instead of attending an over-the-top party. He prefers predictability over surprises. When he does go out for fun, the Introvert can get tired quickly. He can feel a little anxious, overanalyzing what other people think of him or even imagining that they're saying bad things. He's likely to feel exhausted after a long day or night of interactions. It's important to encourage the Introvert to have a healthy social life so that he doesn't recede too far into a solitary world.

Can he commit? After they open up, Introverts make loyal partners. Their sense of security is everything to them, so if they associate you with security, they will cling to you. The Introvert can gift you with intimacy, both emotional and physical. Once he's committed, the Introvert's instinctive sense of secrecy will guarantee that your relationship remains private and free of external influences. In the Introvert's eyes, it will be you and him against the world.

The Introvert can become deeply attached to you if you succeed in breaking through his emotional and mental boundaries. Becoming comfortable with a person and feeling safe enough to share thoughts and ideas is critical to the Introvert. Knowing that you won't hurt him will increase the Introvert's vulnerability, which is what you want. Be careful not to disappoint the Introvert by giving away his secrets or falling short on your promises. He is sensitive, and this can set you back a few giant steps.

Appeal to the Introvert's creativity, as this is a highly imaginative archetype. An Introvert will absorb even the most minute details in his surroundings, noticing things that other people easily miss. If you ever so gently bring his guard down, you can conciliate the Introvert.

What he needs from you: The Introvert's commitment problems are his doubts and inaccessibility. He needs you to give him time to get comfortable. Little by little he'll become less reserved and confess certain things to you about his views of the world and what has happened in his past. But you can't take small progress for granted; if you overwhelm him, the Introvert will retreat into hiding like a turtle snapping back into its shell.

The first thing the Introvert needs to feel from you is trustworthiness. The more he feels at ease with you, the more he will open up. Introverts actually have a million things going on in their minds, although they express very few of their ideas and opinions. You'll discover a whole new side to the Introvert once he's warmed up to you: a playful personality, brilliant mind, and witty sense of humor. The Introvert is highly extroverted around the person he trusts! Granted, you will still need to respect his personal space; this is a must in your relationship with any Introvert.

Compatibility with the Introvert: The Introvert is most compatible with another Introvert and with the Hopeless Romantic. Two Introverts won't force each other to do anything uncomfortable and will appreciate each other's subtlety. Although there is a danger that he'll come on too strongly, the Hopeless Romantic will give the Introvert whatever he or she needs.

CARMEN HARRA, PH.D. AND ALEXANDRA HARRA

There won't be much communication between an Introvert and an Independent because neither will run after the other. An Introvert and a Wounded Warrior won't know what to do for each other because both of these archetypes hide the more profound parts of themselves inside.

Differences between male and female Introverts: The Introverted man might have problems initiating conversation or making plans, both of which men are expected to do. He won't know how to take the lead and that can be a turn off to the woman who likes assertive men. Since he's not aggressive or pushy, he's not considered manly in the typical sense. The Introverted woman may not know how to be firm and stand her ground. She might even be "pushed around" by her partner, especially if he's one of the more strong-willed archetypes like the Narcissist or Workaholic.

Identifying qualities: Closed-off, emotionally guarded, lies by omission, creative, genius, seeks solitude, sensitive, anxious, careful, covert, unresponsive, picky, meticulous, fearful, unconventional way of thinking, obsessive, and compulsive.

Represented by: The fortress. Like a fortress, the Introvert is self-sustainable and closed off to outsiders. He has everything he needs within himself and will only open his doors to those he trusts.

Real-life Introverts: J.K. Rowling, Albert Einstein, and Meryl Streep.

THE IDEAL ARCHETYPE: THE WELL-ROUNDED ONE

Every problem has a solution to the Well-Rounded One, but he won't waste time trying to fix his partner's problems.
—Carmen Harra

We acknowledge that not every reader will find him- or herself within the seven archetypes we outline. If that's the case for you, you may be a Well-Rounded One. Think of the Well-Rounded One as the least problematic and most reasonable kind of partner, an eighth archetype if you will, and what the other archetypes aspire to become: healed, whole, and functional. Keep in mind what you just read about the seven archetypes and compare it to the following description; this is what it feels like to have a partner who embodies stability and a relationship that promotes well-being.

The Well-Rounded One goes beyond what you're looking for in a future partner or what you're hoping your current partner will become—this is what *you're* supposed to become too. You must work to be more well-rounded not for the man you love, or to save your relationship, but for yourself. Before someone else can be this way with you, you have to become a living example of it.

The Well-Rounded One is relatively normal—we use the word *relatively* because no one is completely normal when it comes to relationships; love and attachment can conjure emotions we didn't even know existed! That said, the Well-Rounded One is as normal as it gets: he wants a real relationship and he's mentally and emotionally prepared for it. He can offer commitment without having to surmount the emotional and mental hurdles of the other archetypes. The Well-Rounded One has performed his introspective work, or he might not have significant personality faults to begin with. His barriers are lifted; he is able to give and receive love without impediments.

Any of the archetypes mentioned in this book can become loving, devoted partners if the right actions are taken, yes, but the Well-Rounded One isn't impaired in any area of his life. He's sympathetic to the Wounded Warrior, but he doesn't dwell on the pain of the past. He has needs, but he isn't egoistic like the Narcissist. He's not noticeably introverted or unusually independent. He knows when to step back from his work, unlike the Workaholic. He doesn't hold on to unrealistic notions of love like the Hopeless Romantic. The Well-Rounded One doesn't teeter on the edge of extremes; he'll try hard to find solutions for his relationship problems, but he won't forfeit his well-being for the sake of any partner.

Since the perfect partner doesn't exist, you'll still have to adjust to a relationship with the Well-Rounded One. He can be vulnerable, hurt, reserved, selfish, or ambitious. But what sets him apart is that he's not stuck in being a certain way. Being well-rounded means being versatile, able to adapt to changes and challenges as they come. His number one attribute is his malleability under different circumstances. He's decent in all senses of the word and doesn't have layers of psychological complexities to comb through.

The Well-Rounded One seeks solutions. He leaves no stone unturned in trying to resolve conflict. So if you have an argument with a Well-Rounded One, expect that he'll want to settle it straightaway. He is also not an impulsive man. He doesn't jump to conclusions but takes time to work things out the right way. The Well-Rounded One doesn't rely too heavily on the voices of outsiders, unless that voice is his partner's, whose opinion he values supremely.

Unlike some of the archetypes who have trouble making the right decisions, the Well-Rounded One's conscience is über-developed; his sense of right from wrong is infallible. This is a morally upright man who recognizes when he's transgressed and wants to make it right. Sometimes other people will try to take advantage of his righteousness and make the Well-Rounded One feel guilty in order to get their way. The Well-Rounded Man is patient and tolerant, but don't mistake his kindness for weakness; he can be strong, fierce, and certainly puts his foot down when necessary.

To the Well-Rounded One, life is perfect when it's in balance; he appreciates composure and order more than anyone. His mind is at ease when he has a mission and a sense of purpose. When the Well-Rounded One is under pressure or thrown off course, he becomes introspective; he will retreat into himself to regain his steadiness. He wants a woman who not only complements him but pushes him to become better each day. This is a man who strives for a timeless and enduring relationship, the kind his parents might have had.

Xavier was ready for commitment. He dated and dated but couldn't seem to find someone who truly set his soul on fire. Then Xavier met Elaine, a woman who seemed just as eager for a relationship as he was. The only problem was that Elaine was a Hopeless Romantic archetype, so she came on quite strongly. Because Well-Rounded Ones tend to be great judges of character, Xavier wasn't deterred by Elaine's overenthusiasm; he looked past the fact that she was too sensitive and sacrificial and understood that she had only positive intentions for him. Xavier worked with Elaine to tame her "life equals love" mentality and help her become more realistic and practical. He purposely took their relationship slowly and made Elaine aware of how she was acting every time she became overwhelming. Elaine was receptive to Xavier's guidance and their relationship progressed steadily. Another archetype would have been scared away by Elaine's insistence and need to showcase her love, but Xavier recognized that this was just part of Elaine's way of being and, in the manner of a true Well-Rounded Man, tried to implement solutions instead.

Life experiences are the reason there are so few all-around normal people; the truth is that we've all been hurt, betrayed, or let down, and suffering such trauma destabilizes us, often without our conscious realization. We have witnessed well-rounded clients go from being functional to dysfunctional because the wrong partner came into their lives. Other archetypes can damage the Well-Rounded One: the Narcissist who asked for too much, the Workaholic who didn't pay enough attention, or the Free Spirit who didn't know what he wanted. Cheating on a Well-Rounded Man may turn him into a Wounded Warrior if he doesn't heal or an Introvert if he becomes too closed off. Any well-rounded person can be broken down internally.

Conversely, anyone can become well-rounded by performing the proper work. Take Joe Biden for instance. Whether you support him politically or not, there's no denying the ordeals he passed through in life: losing his first wife and daughter in a car accident, suffering brain aneurysms and blood clots in his lungs during his time in the Senate, and later losing his son, Beau. Biden admits that he was a Wounded Warrior after each tragedy, feeling inconsolable anger and despair. In his first book, *Promises to Keep*, Biden wrote, "I had not known I was capable of such rage… I felt God had played a horrible trick on me." But he was also resilient, as we all are, and fought through each of his battles. During an interview, Biden stated that "Life is a matter of really tough choices." Despite having been heavily wounded, Biden returned to a state of normality and progressed in both his personal and professional ambitions. He realized that holding onto rage or wallowing in misery would not help him in any way, and he chose to relinquish these emotions.

This is what any archetype who evolved into a Well-Rounded One has realized: he has choices. He chose to step forth into the present rather than remain in the past. He chose to heal rather than remain hurt. He chose to open up and trust. And he chose to consider the partner he loves rather than only himself or his work. The Well-Rounded One carefully tends to the emotional wellness he has cultivated, so although he will try to make the relationship work within reasonable means, once he has exhausted his efforts, he will let go of any partner who's proven to be toxic. He enjoys being in control of things, but he must first be in control of himself. His ideal woman completes his mental and emotional equilibrium. To win over the Well-Rounded Man, you must show him that you are as equanimous as he is; he needs a partner to help him maintain his balance. The payoff is that in doing so, you will clear away old habits, emotions, and pains, and become a better person too.

The Well-Rounded One will get along with most of the other archetypes, which is why we didn't include him in the compatibility comparisons. He can make it work with any of the seven, but he is most compatible with another well-rounded person. Two levelheaded people make a highly functional couple. He is least compatible with the Independent, the Free Spirit, and the Narcissist. The Well-Rounded One will feel the Independent and the Free Spirit can't give him a serious relationship and won't waste time trying to convince them otherwise. His character is furthest from the Narcissist and he won't be impressed by the Narcissist's conceitedness.

April was a Well-Rounded Woman, always on top of things and in control of her life. She met Pierre and the two hit it off immediately. Pierre was funny and charming—his energy was magnetic. April and Pierre started going out together and having lots of fun, something that had been missing from April's life. But April soon noticed that Pierre had certain inclinations she didn't like: he was very much into himself. And this was not the only problem—Pierre wasn't taking into consideration April's needs or desires. To her it seemed that it was either Pierre's way or no way at all. Everything had to be on Pierre's time and terms. Pierre claimed that he was quite fond of April, yet he rarely asked about how she was feeling or how her day was going. In fact, he mostly spoke about himself. April liked Pierre, a low-grade Narcissist; he was a nice guy and she was developing serious feelings for him. But April wasn't willing to jeopardize her sense of self for anyone. So she chose to let him go. The Well-Rounded One prefers to walk away if you show him that you're self-absorbed, unrealistic, or covert and are unwilling to work on such tendencies.

The Well-Rounded One likes to commit to people he deems capable of commitment. Unlike the Narcissist, who seizes the day for all its worth, the Well-Rounded One regards his life in the long term, weighing carefully the possible outcomes for each of his decisions. The Well-Rounded One has a thorough understanding of human nature. If he sees that you have trouble keeping a job or friendships, he'll assume you'll have trouble keeping a relationship with him too. He protects himself, but not in an ego-induced way like the Narcissist; he simply wants to have a partner who can contribute to the mental, emotional, and physical stability he's worked so hard to attain. So the Well-Rounded One wants to know that you're *whole* in all senses of the word: in your other relationships, in your emotions, and in your actions. The Well-Rounded One appreciates reliability because he's a man of his word, so to make him commit, you'll have to show him that you not only talk the talk but walk the walk. Self-control is the golden ticket to the Well-Rounded Man's heart: be open with him without throwing yourself at him, take the relationship seriously but don't rush into things, and be respectable without seeming prudish.

Sound too good to be true? Many women don't believe that such a man even exists! We've noticed that many of our female clients are skeptical when they meet a "normal" guy. They think, *Okay, what's the catch? What's wrong with him?* Women who have suffered through bad experiences in love presume that every man will disappoint them sooner or later. But trust us when we say that there are plenty of well-rounded partners out there, looking for their better, equally balanced half. And if your love interest now isn't that well-rounded and fits the description of one of the more complicated archetypes, rest assured that willpower can work miracles.

Chapter 8

YOU WILL GET THE LOVE
YOU DESERVE

All things become possible in the presence of love.
—Alexandra Harra

So you've figured out your partner's archetype and learned all about it—now what? Now it's time to get down to the nitty-gritty of your relationship: the work! There's no getting around the fact that all relationships require a substantial amount of work (more so in this day and age). We know you didn't want to hear that; it would be heavenly to meet the right person and automatically go on autopilot, but relationships can't meet their full potential that way.

In our final chapter, we offer an extensive relationship wrap-up. We'll cover compatibility on all levels of being and give away the secrets to creating emotional intimacy. We'll also give you solutions to common and not-so-common relationship problems and a few affirmations to strengthen your bond with your loved one. That way, you're prepared to navigate through any obstacle that stands in the way of getting the love you deserve.

THE UNIVERSAL LAW OF COMPATIBILITY

Before commitment comes chemistry, the initial force that attracts you to one another. While it's true that some archetypes "match" better with others, compatibility is a universal law that applies to *all* enduring relationships. Many people, however, have a skewed perception of what it means to be a match. Compatibility isn't looking into each other's eyes and seeing stars; it's seeing the same stars when you look up at the night sky—seeing the world with the same eyes.

We hear our clients say, "I felt chemistry right away," or, "We're totally compatible." When we ask them to define what they mean by chemistry or compatibility, they answer something along the lines of, "You know, that *spark*." And by "spark" they mean getting along without effort, sharing a laugh, or holding a meaningful conversation. We can all agree that chemistry feels like internal fireworks going off, but we also know that fireworks fizzle out quickly. And when they wear out, what will remain?

Sharing chemistry is fun, not to mention necessary. But it isn't indicative of a person's capacity to remain loyal or devoted, especially in time. No matter your partner's archetype, genuine chemistry is measured by the values you hold in common. True compatibility is sharing similar life goals and beliefs about commitment. These must match so that you can evolve together, not apart.

One of these beliefs has to do with the way you handle arguments. It's unrealistic to think that your relationship won't be subject to any sort of conflict; conflict is inevitable and must be addressed. What matters most is how you move past it. But if you both need to be right all the time, your disagreements will never cease. If you both need to talk over each other to get your points across, your neighbors will eventually call the police because of all the shouting.

Knowing how to compromise on your disagreements is much more useful than always being in agreement. Specifically, you both have to be willing to commit to your differences as much as you commit to your commonalities. You don't have to have the same religion, background, or upbringing as your partner, because compatibility is being able to say, "To each his own," and accepting the discrepancies between you. Compromise is the happy medium that keeps two people together for the long run. Make sure that, regardless of his archetype, the person you choose to spend your life with is willing to put aside differences to keep the relationship in good standing.

Being able to apologize is also a big factor in compatibility. If you refuse to admit fault and your partner refuses to admit fault, you're both refusing to resolve a problem. Both sides must be willing to say "I'm sorry" as often as needed. You won't be able to keep up a relationship with a person who's unwilling to budge from his position.

This becomes particularly important if and when you choose to start a family, as both parents have to share one parenting style. The more you see eye to eye with your partner, the more you can agree on bigger issues and raise your children without dissension. Even when one parent disagrees with the other, he still has to back his partner up in front of their children. Your kids will respect you more as parents if they see that you're able to co-parent smoothly. Make sure that you and your partner can apply the same methods when it comes to your children.

As much as compatibility is felt within, it exists on the material side of your relationship too, so your earning and spending habits must match from the beginning. It will pose many problems if one partner likes to save his hard-earned money while the other loves to blow it away on luxuries or if one partner has to pay everything for the other. Both partners have to be on the same page in terms of saving and investing. Make sure you understand the limitations of your partner's career and find out whether he has a backup plan. As financial expert Suze Orman said, "Opposites attract, but I wouldn't bet my money on financial opposites."

Having parallel views about work and money will help you spend more time together, which is essential to keep up compatibility. If your partner works at night and you work during the day, understand that this will cause problems. Or if your partner is always busy and has no time to spend with you, you won't feel like you're in much of a relationship. When it comes to the notion of time, you have to run on the same clock or be able to set aside days to spend together.

And when you are together, if you're compatible you'll show each other the same level of affection. Emotionally speaking, one partner shouldn't be warm while the other is cold. The attention you give should be given to you too. It's a mark of incompatibility when one person is always giving love and affection that's not reciprocated.

Another inconvenient truth about compatibility is that people change over time. When you first meet your partner, he might be on the same path as you. He might like all of the things you like and have the same hobbies you have, making you think, *Wow, this is great, we have so many things in common!* But in one, five, or ten years from the time you meet, he might not like *any* of those things anymore. And you might not either. You could grow to have separate tastes and want to do different things. Perceptions shift, and your partner can literally transform into a new person. What then? You'll find yourself asking, "Where is the man I fell in love with?"

This is why you have to compensate for each other's weaknesses; what he lacks, you have, and vice versa. If you're good at managing time but your partner isn't, you can help him organize his schedule and be punctual. And if he's good at saving money but you're not, he can help you balance your checkbook and cut down on unnecessary spending. Alone, you're incomplete, but together, you're supposed to be whole. If you're both lacking in the same areas, you aren't complementary. You'll experience the same problems over and over again because neither partner will be able to compensate for what the other doesn't have.

Be careful of being with a person who has a tendency to bring up what you lack, what you're not good at, or what you're sensitive about every time you get into an argument. A certain level of respect must be upheld within your relationship at all times. Even with the patient of a saint, any woman will reach a breaking point and either lash out or leave if she's constantly disrespected by her partner.

Authentic compatibility transcends personality types. It's a deep-seated connection that survives in time because it's grounded in life principles. Now that you understand the crux of compatibility, let's learn how to initiate more intimacy.

SECRETS TO EMOTIONAL INTIMACY

*Being emotionally intimate with your partner
means being in touch with his soul.*
—Alexandra Harra

What brings two people together is chemistry, but what keeps them together is emotional intimacy. Intimacy isn't restricted to intercourse; it's intense bonding of the mind and spirit too. It is knowing what your partner needs before he even gets a chance to ask—feeling his emotions, needs, and desires as if they were your own. There is something so simple yet so joyful about knowing your partner this deeply. When two people share emotional intimacy, the effects of even the most insignificant actions are intensified; a touch of the hand can feel like heaven!

Emotional intimacy is much more powerful than physical intimacy because it delves deep into your loved one's fears and hopes. It reaches far beyond age, appearance, or social status. These things alter with time and won't keep a couple together. You may be physically attracted to someone, or tempted by his money or power, but only when you hold an intimate conversation with that person can you grasp his way of thinking.

Being consistently *aware* of your partner is key. Maintain a sense of intimacy with him by paying attention to how he's behaving on a day-to-day basis. What's bothering him? What can you do to relieve his worries? Recognize what it is that your partner needs most from you in that given moment—is it to be nurtured or left alone? Acknowledging your significant other's needs will keep you perfectly in tune as a couple. And making tiny sacrifices that mean the world to him will generate greater intimacy. When there exists emotional intimacy, two people vibrate on the same level spiritually, even if they're in different places physically. You can be telepathically intimate with someone who's a thousand miles away, literally sensing if something has happened or if he isn't feeling well. If two partners don't share sentimental symmetry, their relationship potential is limited.

We can become emotionally immune to our partner over time as monotony sets in and boredom strikes. Scientifically speaking, dopamine levels in the brain drop as we get used to a person. Most couples simply stand by and allow the spark of their relationship to die out or look for it elsewhere, partly because they believe there's nothing they can do. But with the right actions, both partners can reignite the romantic fire so that it burns even more strongly than in the beginning.

Feelings of exhilaration can be rekindled through new and old activities. Push your partner and yourself out of your comfort zones. To start, go back to the beginning and do something you loved to do in the first few months of your relationship. Leave the cell phones at home and communicate throughout the activity. Then, try something completely new, something you've always wanted to try but perhaps haven't had time. There are no excuses to doing whatever it takes to keep love alive.

You can develop emotional intimacy with your partner through daily activities like joint visualizations. With time, this will help you grow closer. Skillful daydreaming is a fine spiritual tool. Many people use visualization exercises to empower themselves in the real world. You already do this with your partner whenever you plan or envision your future together.

Take it one step further. Hold your partner's hand and take turns speaking your dreams into existence. You can say things like, "I see us walking into our new home. It's a brick house with a garden in front," or whatever it is you both want to attain. Make it a nightly or weekly habit. Joint visualizations inspire you to work toward mutual objectives.

While doing this, you can reinforce your love through speech. Never underestimate the power of the right words to improve your dynamic. There are two ways to say "I love you," halfheartedly and wholeheartedly. When you tell your partner you love him, mean it and demonstrate the passion behind your words. This means speaking a full and excited "I love you" instead of a hurried "love ya." Reiterate his value in your life. Hold your partner close and experience every inch of his being: smell his hair, feel his bare back, and hear his heart beat. Close your eyes and tell him what he means to you. Compliment and empower him. Don't think too much; speak from the seat of your soul.

Watch your partner's body language as you speak. Pay attention to his breathing, when he sighs, if he crosses his legs, where he holds his hands, etc. Most movements are subconscious, but every single one is for a reason. When you note small movements, you can decipher your partner's comfort level and figure out what makes him feel uneasy. In time, you can come to know what your partner is thinking just by watching the way he holds himself.

It also helps to make eye contact to magnify your connection. There may be times when you want to avoid looking your partner in the eye, like when he's made you upset. Even in these moments, keep in mind that nothing is as effective at conveying (or betraying!) sentiments as eye contact. Words may reach the brain, but a glance trickles down to the soul. Practice looking your partner in the eye when you address him to heighten the potency of your words.

Engage in quality conversation too. This includes holding mindful dialogue with your partner. Anyone can communicate, but not everyone can communicate effectively, which is why we stress the word *quality* here. Complain less and ask more. Ask questions that are important to your partner to help him open up, but don't make the conversation seem like an interview. Ask one relevant question, then let him talk as much (or as little) as he wants. Listen to his choice of words and his hesitation at certain moments; such actions reveal subconscious emotions. He may be trying to tell you how something makes him feel but may have trouble getting it out. Consider the caliber of your conversations: are you speaking enough, and if so, what is the basis of your talks? Are you reaching helpful conclusions together or harmful conclusions about each other? The right kind of speech can be remarkably healing, as it offers a brand-new perspective and moves you closer to a resolution. When all else fails, simply ask, "How are you feeling today?" or, "How do you feel about (subject)?" We'll give you more tips to successful communication in the following section.

An honest exchange opens the channels of emotional flow. Normally, we caution our female clients about being too emotional in their relationship, and we advise our male clients to be more emotional with their partners. Negative emotions like rage, contempt, or hate should be subdued for the sake of your relationship, but positive emotions must be experienced in their totality. Joy, passion, pleasure, and comfort—these feelings should be expressed without restraint. Relinquish your fear of being too vulnerable and simply allow yourself to feel.

Far surpassing physical intimacy, emotional intimacy fosters durability, harmony, and stability between partners. Use these secrets to establish the foundation for a strong and intimate relationship.

CHALLENGES YOU'LL FACE AND SOLUTIONS YOU CAN APPLY

The most effective step you can take to conquer relationship challenges is to change your attitude: seeing things in a new light can shift the energy of a situation entirely. As we're sure you know by now, your brain resorts to the same thoughts over and over again. Reducing discord in relationships starts by rearranging your thoughts. When you consciously control harmful thoughts and replace them with more positive ones, your relationship transforms. Concentrating on more elevated thoughts will lead you to speak and act differently, which will yield different results from your partner. This is not to say that you'll have to let him be right all the time, or give up what's fair to you, but that you'll have to try new approaches in dealing with old problems. Commitment is a daily choice; every day, you can choose to act in ways that encourage or discourage love.

Some relationships can take years to build and only minutes to break. Circumstances (often beyond our control) wear out even the most blissful relationships. It's a consequence of all long-term relationships: things aren't the same as they were in the beginning. But this process, ironically, can also strengthen your relationship, because the more you overcome together, the stronger you become together. The good news is that as long as love exists, there is a solution for every conceivable relationship problem—common, uncommon, and convoluted. In the following section, we highlight some of the challenges all relationships will face sooner or later, and the actions required to keep commitment strong. Think of them as the "how-tos" of your relationship:

Quality, not quantity. From this point forward, start to measure your relationship in terms of quality, not quantity—the value, not the amount. You don't need a dozen meaningless talks to heal whatever damage was done; you need one transformative conversation. You don't have to have sex every day, so long as you're both satisfied when you do have intercourse. You don't need your partner to spend every waking moment with you; you need to enjoy the time you do spend together. Like a meticulously built house, every element in your relationship should be high in quality.

Communicate, don't interrogate. Most couples complain of communication issues. Lack of communication is a common problem in relationships because people tend to hold on to their egos and opinions a little too dearly. But it's a roadblock that seriously impedes progress: if you're not talking openly and sincerely, how can you know what your partner wants? How can you come up with solutions?

There are right and wrong ways to communicate. The wrong way is bombarding your partner with all of your problems as soon as he walks through the door after a long day at work. The right way is waiting until he unwinds and then gently bringing up one subject of genuine concern (*one* subject, not twenty). Ask about his day before you begin. You might feel an urge to bring up everything at once when expressing how you feel, but it's best to stick to one topic.

You will get to cover all the crucial points in time, so start with the most pertinent. Listen intently when he opens up to you. Don't jump from subject to subject or concentrate on irrelevant matters that don't pose serious problems. If you communicate aggressively, your partner will respond in kind. He's more likely to be receptive if you're already engaged in a comfortable conversation.

The timing of a conversation is of equal importance as the topic. Make sure his emotions are settled and steady before embarking on a subject you're keen to discuss, and make sure yours are too. We understand you want to get things off your chest right now, but you have to respect your partner's time or the conversation won't turn out the way you want. Know when to have the serious talks and when to wait. If your partner is in a compromised mood because he just got bad news, it's better to wait a couple hours or even a few days. However, if your partner is showing emotional vulnerability, seize the moment: capitalize on the times when he's feeling sensitive, impartial, and loving. These are your best moments to say what you need to say, as he will be most open-minded.

Think, don't act. Acting on the first emotions you feel can hurt you and your partner greatly, especially if those emotions are aggressive or irrational. Speaking out of anger or doing things for the wrong reasons hinders both your personal progress and progress with your partner. Tame your emotions so that instead of reacting immediately, you first weigh the effects your actions could have in the short and long terms. Always ask yourself, "If I do this, how could it play out?" Explore all possibilities. Scribble down your thoughts and return to the conversation after you've calmed down. We want you to think before you act from now on, not just in your relationships but in every area of life.

Adventure, not routine. The daily grind becomes boring, to say the least. Doing the same things every day can quickly kill the spirit of any relationship, no matter how close the partners may be. Break out of routine as often as you can. Travel with your partner, even if it's a road trip or a weekend getaway. Try new restaurants and take up new hobbies. Even if it's something out of your comfort zone, find joy in the fact that you're engaging in different activities with your other half.

This also holds true in the bedroom. Many men and women find that their sex drive dwindles after years of being with the same person; the "rush" that accompanies intercourse fades. While this is normal, it's not a good indication. Good sex is an integral part of any relationship. If desire dries up, a central component of your connection is lost. Strive to maintain your sex appeal for your lover. Eat well and exercise regularly. Such activities will not only help you look good for him, they'll make you feel good about yourself and boost your self-esteem too! Sex can become better with time if you get creative and invent new ways of pleasing each other. Be a little daring and try intercourse in different locations and positions or order an erotic movie to enjoy together.

Simplify, don't complicate. We often forget that in love, simplicity is key. Naturally, we want to build an empire with our partner, but in doing so, we can lose sight of the simple values that first fostered love. Return to simplicity. Nothing is more valuable at the end of the day than tender moments shared in silence, with no mention of what was, could have been, or might be. Declutter your relationship. Clear out toxicity like harmful emotions and hurtful memories. Maintain a love as pure as water.

Create, don't destroy. Many relationships are slowly created and quickly destroyed. Hold sacred the principle of creation. As a rule of thumb, if it survives, help it thrive. This includes not just our natural world—which we should be helping to preserve—but ideas and projects that your partner has brought to life. Don't destroy his esteem, demolish his hope, or sabotage his well-being. Give birth to healthy habits, thoughts, and goals with your partner. Sustain the creation of beautiful things throughout your relationship.

We, not me. The ego is the most destructive force in relationships. It tears down human bonds because it favors the *me* and neglects the *we*. This is why archetypes in the "me" category tend to have shorter relationships than archetypes in the "we" category. For the sake of your relationship, let your proud guard down. Take nothing personal. Even if your partner does something irrefutably wrong, recognize that he may have personal issues that you know nothing about and that also have nothing to do with you. Realize that in relationships, everything is compromise, sacrifice, and endurance. Hold your partner closer to your heart than you hold your own ego, and you'll succeed in holding a healthy, long-term relationship.

Strengths, not weaknesses. You have the choice to focus on your partner's strengths or weaknesses—to build him up or tear him down to nothing. In reality, you hold more power than you can imagine! Remember that weaknesses are far more visible than strengths, but that it's a sign of personal weakness to play on the shortcomings of another person. You may joke to others about your loved one's imperfections and think it's no big deal, but this can be extremely hurtful to him. Refrain from speaking negatively about your significant other in public. You may want to vent to others, but keeping quiet is wiser. Instead of starting the day by scolding your partner, begin your day by thanking him: "Thank you for being next to me through everything. Thank you for being you." Nurture the person who has stood by you; he is more sensitive than you know. Tolerate his defects as you tolerate your own. A simple "I'm proud of you" can light up your partner's entire day.

Responsibility, not blame. Taking responsibility is a step you can't skip over if you want to have peace in your relationship. You'll have to assume responsibility for any role you might've played in bringing about a problem. It's easy to place the blame entirely on your partner, but faultfinding only worsens the situation. So instead of pointing fingers, peer within. Even if you did absolutely nothing wrong, consider what you can do to make things right next time.

Meditation, not desperation. Fights often happen because one or both partners have become desperate; bickering emerges from dissatisfactions that were never addressed. It's essential to organize your thoughts and intentions before you open your mouth. Even if you feel you're at your wit's end, sit down and meditate on it. Consider what would happen if you approached the situation with greater calm and more logic. Imagine the best possible outcome in your mind. See yourself having an honest conversation with your partner in which you reach an agreement that's satisfactory to both of you. Plan the points you will make. What can you say to inspire a solution? Meditation helps you access your higher self, where all solutions are available to you.

Reception, not reaction. Hearing and listening are two separate arts. No one starts an argument to listen to the other person's opinion; we want to get our own points across. Our first instinct is to react to confrontation right away: our partner makes a claim, we make a counterclaim, and this starts a back and forth that quickly goes downhill. One of the keys to being receptive is to invite your partner to talk first. Ask him a question that's likely to make him release his thoughts and feelings. Listen to your partner without interrupting and without planning an entire lecture in response. Then, you can tell him that you're ready to share your point of view. Speak to him like you speak to your best friend: uninhibited and unintimidated. When you learn to listen, the quality of your conversations will improve. And when words can cause irreparable harm, silence is golden. Absorbing the true meaning of your partner's words can take time, so go over what he said in your mind before you form a conclusion. As Voltaire said, "The ear is the avenue to the heart."

Present, not past. Living outside of time disempowers you; living in the now endows you with strength. When you give up expectations that are disadvantageous, you start to live in the present and treasure the time you spend with your partner to the fullest. You no longer worry about what he has to do or how he has to change according to you because you become more accepting of your differences. When you embrace the present, you're focused on making the best of whatever situation you're faced with at the moment. You harness the full might of your power and the resources you're given. When you find your thoughts drifting to what could've been or what might be, stop them and return to the present. Center yourself by taking several deep breaths and becoming aware of your surroundings: what do you smell, feel, hear, taste, and see? Take note of the date and time: you and your loved one exist here and now. Developing a healthy relationship with the notion of time grants you peace of mind.

Start each day with a clean slate. Even if your partner messed up yesterday, there's no reason he can't make up for his mistakes tomorrow. Focus not on what he's done wrong but on the opportunity to do right from now on. Yes, people can change, but you must give them the chance.

Needs, not desires. Be specific about your needs, not your desires. You might crave a vacation with your better half but strictly speaking, this is not a need. The actual need is to spend time with him, whether on an island or in your home. Identify the core of what's driving your desires. Understand what sacrifices will be needed from both you and your partner in order to fulfill each other's needs. Remember that your significant other has needs from you too.

Purpose, not pointless. You shouldn't be doing things in your relationship "just because." Don't bring up old, irrelevant topics just because they popped up in your mind or interrogate about events that happened years ago because you're bored. Stick to what matters now. Everything you do think, say, and do should be founded in purpose: for the purpose of bringing you closer and advancing your relationship.

Intimacy, not influence. Keep your relationship exclusive and guard your privacy. External influences are the weeds that ruin a flourishing bond. We invite all sorts of energies into our relationship without even noticing: family, friends, and enemies all play a role in the fluctuating energy we share with our partner. We like to believe that people wish us well when sometimes they don't. Be aware of who and what is interfering in your relationship. Don't do things like hang up on your boyfriend in the middle of a conversation then call your friend to complain about him. It is you and your partner who are in a relationship, not your friend, sibling, parent, or any other party. Promise to put each other first and filter out negative influences.

Reality, not perfection. The love we know we deserve sometimes differs from the love we actually receive. Why is that? Part of the reason is that people are far from perfect. They won't always give us what we want; rather, they'll give us what they *can*. Not everyone is capable of extending unconditional love, patience, and tolerance. While you should never lower your expectations or settle for less than what you deserve, you should acknowledge your partner's limitations and recognize his true capacity. Maybe he's already giving you everything he can.

Literally, not personally. When we care about a person, we can become overly sensitive to the things he says and does. We can twist his intentions and make ourselves believe bad things he didn't even mean. The way your partner treats you says much more about him than it says about you. He may be going through things you can't comprehend—mentally, emotionally, or physically—so take nothing personally.

Source, not consequence. Dig down to the first rotten seed of your relationship. When and why did the fighting start? Say you've been arguing about the lack of time you spend together. Pinpoint the origin of the problem instead of the ramifications it's having. The source might be your partner's demanding job, while the consequence is that he missed your birthday. In this example, arguing about the missed birthday won't stop the problem from happening again, but strategizing how your partner can reorganize his schedule or take a few days off will. Remember that the outcome can't change if the cause doesn't.

Resolutions, not conclusions. It's all too easy to jump to conclusions. When something goes wrong, we automatically assume the worst and analyze every part of our partner's actions. Frustrations accumulate, and people reach their boiling points without a way to process their emotions. This kind of impulsivity causes irreversible damage and breeds more problems.

The most critical part of any fight is the way you make up: what's the resolution, and who's benefiting from it? Arguments can be quite productive if the conclusions you reach outweigh the dispute. Never leave quarrels unfinished or let things "go away on their own." An argument that happens once is bound to become a recurring problem. Compromise to resolve disagreements once and for all by eliminating the core of your hostility. The aim is to reach an understanding with your partner in which petty feuds are averted and long-standing arguments are settled. Skip the would'ves, should'ves, and could'ves, and ask, "So how do we fix this?" Offer possible solutions and invite your partner to provide his input.

Evolution, not change. People are constantly changing. You're not the same person you were last year, last month, or even last week. Unlike a teenager passing through puberty, you won't be able to look in a mirror and see your changes; they won't always be obvious. And it's even easier to become oblivious to your partner's changes since you're with him every day.

Register the ways in which your loved one is evolving and adapt yourself to him. In the case of physical change, make it known to your partner that you notice the new look. Always compliment a different hairstyle, weight loss, a fresh wardrobe, etc. Remain well ahead of changes by preparing for the next phase of your relationship and strategizing how you'll pass through it side by side.

While you should be optimistic about your future with your partner, you should also remain aware of the ways in which his commitment to you is likely to change through time. Increased responsibilities like kids, a house, and bills make it difficult to maintain an ideal relationship. How will you and your partner respond to challenges as they arise? We said before that the way we face our problems often reveals our true nature.

The evolution of your relationship is a two-way street. Both partners have to be in agreement and want to move in the same direction. Progress requires a conscious desire to change. And the most powerful way to facilitate change in another person is to change yourself. If your partner won't budge, consider modifying your own behavior. Understand what actions you need to take to improve the dynamic between you. Once you make the necessary changes, your partner will react in one way or another.

You should also be asking yourself this question regularly: "Is my relationship evolving or only changing?" A relationship should not only shift but shift positively over time as both partners work to break through impasses. Evolve alongside your significant other. If this is not happening, it's time to evaluate at which point the relationship became stagnant and how it can be revived.

The art of human connections comes from these simple principles that reduce discord and increase attachment. Recurring conflicts can come to an end by adjusting your attitude to reshape your relationship.

AFFIRMATIONS TO EMPOWER
YOUR RELATIONSHIP

You can practice these affirmations alone or with your partner to fortify your relationship and enact trust between you.

I love my partner wholeheartedly; I accept his flaws as I accept my own.

Alone, my partner and I are imperfect. Together, we are whole and complete.

Today, we choose to keep out external influences and work through our relationship on our own.

My partner and I are inseparable from each other and emotionally intimate with one another.

I forgive my partner's mistakes and I know that he has learned from them; I trust him fully.

It doesn't matter what tomorrow brings; I'm happy with my partner in the present moment.

My partner and I offer the highest versions of ourselves to each other.

My partner and I share an unbreakable bond.

Each day, I grow more grateful that I'm able to share my life with a wonderful person.

A FINAL WORD ON COMMITMENT

You were meant to pick up this book, dear reader, because you're at a time in your life when you're ready to redefine what commitment means for you. True commitment delivers life's most precious treasures: absolute fulfillment and inner harmony.

Commitment starts and ends with you; your first commitment must be to yourself, for yourself, and by yourself. When you tend to your well-being on all levels, the channels of commitment open with ease.

The value of commitment grows if cultivated. Like flowers in a garden, love blossoms when it's well cared for. Any archetype can transform and thrive in a lifelong relationship if you believe in him and apply the right approach.

Believe that you deserve commitment, because you do. Believe that you deserve joy, because you do. Believe that you deserve unconditional, eternal, omnipotent love, because you do. All that you believe you will receive, because that is how the universe works.

The right kind of love can and will change your life. Whether you're in a relationship or you're searching for the right companion, whether you've been hurt more times than you can count or you've lost hope that good people exist, or whether you run into the same problems with your partner or you can't seem to make peace with yourself, choose to continue believing in the almighty power of love. It is the only force that heals, supports, and makes whole.

Lord Tennyson put it best: "Love is the only gold."

ACKNOWLEDGMENTS

We would like to thank Sanda, Victor, and Virgil, our three guardian angels who continue to inspire us with timeless wisdom to guide others toward their best lives.

Also by Carmen Harra, Ph.D.

The Karma Queens' Guide to Relationships: The Truth about Karma and Relationships (with Alexandra Harra)

Wholeliness: Embracing the Sacred Unity That Heals Our World

Decoding Your Destiny

The Eleven Eternal Principles: Accessing the Divine Within

Everyday Karma: A Renowned Psychic Shows You How to Change Your Life by Changing Your Karma

The Trinity of Health: Align Body, Mind and Soul in Order to Achieve Health and Happiness for Your Whole Life

ABOUT THE AUTHORS

Carmen Harra, Ph.D., is an intuitive psychologist, best-selling author, radio show host, TV personality, and relationship expert. Over the past twenty-five years, Carmen has helped tens of thousands of people find fulfilling love and create committed relationships. She's the author of international best-selling books like *Everyday Karma*, *Decoding Your Destiny*, and *The Karma Queens' Guide to Relationships*, among others. Carmen has been featured in such publications as *The New York Times*, *New York Post*, and *New York Daily News* and on shows like *Good Morning America*, *The View*, and the *Today* show. She contributes regularly to *HuffPost*, *Thrive Global*, *Sivana East*, *Bustle*, and many more popular magazines. Visit her website at www.CarmenHarra.com.

Alexandra Harra is a certified relationship coach, professional writer, and cover model. She holds BAs in creative writing and classics and has been featured on numerous TV shows and in publications around the world.